START EXPLORING™
INSECTS
A FACT-FILLED COLORING BOOK

George S. Glenn, Jr.
Illustrated by Helen I. Driggs

RUNNING PRESS

PHILADELPHIA, PENNSYLVANIA

Canadian representatives: General Publishing Co., Ltd.,
30 Lesmill Road, Don Mills, Ontario M3B 2T6.

International representatives: Worldwide Media Services, Inc.,
30 Montgomery Street, Jersey City, New Jersey 07302.

9 8 7 6 5 4 3 2

Digit on the right indicates the number of this printing.

ISBN 1-56138-043-1

Editorial Director: Nancy Steele
Editor: Gregory C. Aaron
Cover design: Toby Schmidt
Interior design: Jacqueline Spadaro
Cover, interior, and poster illustrations: Helen I. Driggs
Poster copyright © 1991 Running Press Book Publishers
Typography: CG Century Oldstyle with ITC Franklin Gothic Heavy,
by COMMCOR Communications Corporation, Philadelphia, Pennsylvania

*Insects are helpful creatures, but remember to always treat them with respect.
The author and publishers are not responsible for any accidents or injuries arising
from the use of the information in this book.*

This book may be ordered by mail from the publisher.
Please add $2.50 for postage and handling.
But try your bookstore first!
Running Press Book Publishers
125 South Twenty-second Street
Philadelphia, Pennsylvania 19103.

CONTENTS

INTRODUCTION
The Age of Insects

Many different kinds of creatures have roamed the earth since the dawn of life. Some have been more successful than others. For example, great lizards ruled the earth one hundred million years ago. That's why we call that time the Age of Dinosaurs. Some people say that today we are in the Age of Mammals or the Age of Man. But if we select the kind of creature that exists in the greatest numbers and variety, we should call our time the Age of Insects.

If you look, you'll discover more insects than any other type of living creature. There seem to be more mosquitoes than birds, more butterflies than buffalo, even more roaches than rats. Not only can you find multitudes of insects near your home, but scientists have also discovered tens of thousands of different kinds of insects living in the tropical rain forests of the world.

Almost two million kinds, or *species* (SPEE-sheez), of plants and animals have been discovered and described. Half of all these species are insects. Scientists discover new species all the time as they explore the great wealth of insect life in South America, Africa, and southeast Asia. Estimates of the number of insect species have grown with time. Ancient Greek scientists guessed that there were 1,000 species. Now *entomologists* (EN-tuh-MOL-uh-jists), the scientists who study insects, think there may be ten million (10,000,000) species or more! In the United States alone, almost 100,000 species of insects have been recorded. How many do you think you've seen near your home?

Though small, insects are an important part of the environment. Bees, flies, wasps, ants, and butterflies help plants to produce seed and fruit by pollinating their flowers. They also clean up dead plant and animal matter. And insects are important food for many animals. Spiders build webs to snag grasshoppers, bats hunt for flying moths, birds dine on caterpillars, and fish nibble on mosquitoes.

To survive this perilous world, insects practice successful survival techniques. Insects imitate leaves and stones, spray poisons, raid other insects, farm food, hitchhike thousands of miles, transmit silent songs, and even cooperate with one another. These incredible insect talents—and many others—are explained in the following pages. To discover more, just color the pictures and read about the amazing lives of insects.

Ancient Insects

The Age of Insects extends far back in time—even before the arrival of dinosaurs. As with the great reptiles, evidence of ancient insects is found in fossils. The oldest insect fossils are 400 to 440 million years old. These first insects were wingless and looked very much like the common silverfish and springtails of today. The first flying insects appeared about 300 million years ago, a period when great swamp forests of giant ferns, horsetails, and club mosses covered wide areas of the world. In these forests, large dragonflies, roaches, and roach-like insects flew and scampered.

With the arrival of flowering plants, insect variety increased. Bees, wasps, flies, and butterflies evolved and used these plants for food.

The picture of ancient insect development is incomplete. Insect bodies are small and fragile, so insect fossils are scarce. Most fossils have been found in shale and limestone. Perhaps the most exciting fossils have been found in a remarkable stone called *amber*. Originally, amber was sticky sap that oozed from trees millions of years ago. It trapped insects, spiders, and scorpions in a transparent yellow goo. The sap hardened over time, preserving the creatures inside.

Insects trapped in amber are often completely intact and can be easily seen through the clear yellow stone. These ancient insects are so well-preserved that scientists can study their muscles and the insides of their bodies. Many extinct species of insects have been preserved for us in amber.

Even though millions of years have passed, many insects look much as they did in prehistoric times. This long history of insects indicates that insects are the most successful animals ever to roam the land. If you don't believe it, just ask a dinosaur.

TIME FOR INSECTS

Here's how long ago these animals appeared in the world:

FISH	COCKROACHES	DRAGONFLIES	BEETLES	DINOSAURS	GRASSHOPPERS AND WASPS	MAMMALS	BIRDS	DINOSAURS DIE OUT	BUTTERFLIES	EARLY WHALES	FLEAS	EARLY HUMANS	MODERN HUMANS
400 MILLION	360 MILLION	300 MILLION	260 MILLION	225 MILLION	200 MILLION	180 MILLION	150 MILLION	65 MILLION	60 MILLION	50 MILLION	40 MILLION	1.5 MILLION	40,000

YEARS AGO

In the Age of Dinosaurs, dragonflies had wings that measured two feet (.6 meter) from tip to tip!

Ordering the Insects

The world has millions of species of plants and animals, and thousands upon thousands of insect species. To name and describe all these amazingly different forms of life, scientists have created a "family tree" containing every species ever discovered. They have organized the animal kingdom by showing similarities and differences in the way animal bodies are put together.

Insects are members of a larger group of animals called *arthropods,* a word that means "jointed feet." This group of insect relatives includes scorpions, crabs, centipedes, millipedes, and spiders. All these animals have jointed legs and bodies. Insects are arthropods with three body segments, one set of antennae, and six legs. These features set them apart from the other arthropods, which have different numbers of body segments and legs. For example, spiders are arthropods too, but spiders all have eight legs and two body segments. These differences set spiders apart from insects.

The insect world has twenty-nine divisions called orders. Each order contains species which resemble each other in a specific way. For instance, all insects with two wings (flies and mosquitoes) belong to the order Diptera.

Every species has been given a unique name so it can't be confused with another species. Each scientific name has two parts. For example, humans are called *Homo sapiens* (which means "wise man"), and alfalfa butterflies are called *Colias eurytheme*. All scientific names are in Latin. Having all the names in the same language makes it easy for scientists around the world to trade information.

When an entomologist thinks he or she has discovered a new species of insect, the classification system helps show what other species the new one is related to. Other entomologists help confirm the new discovery. Then the discoverer gets to choose the scientific name that the new species will be known by.

BE TRUE TO BUGS

Most people use the word "bug" to mean any insect. But technically, only some insects are bugs. "True bugs" are insects of the order Hemiptera. Most have oval-shaped bodies. Here are some true bugs:

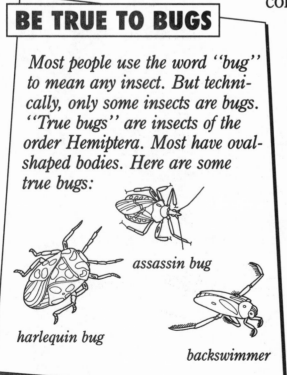

assassin bug

harlequin bug

backswimmer

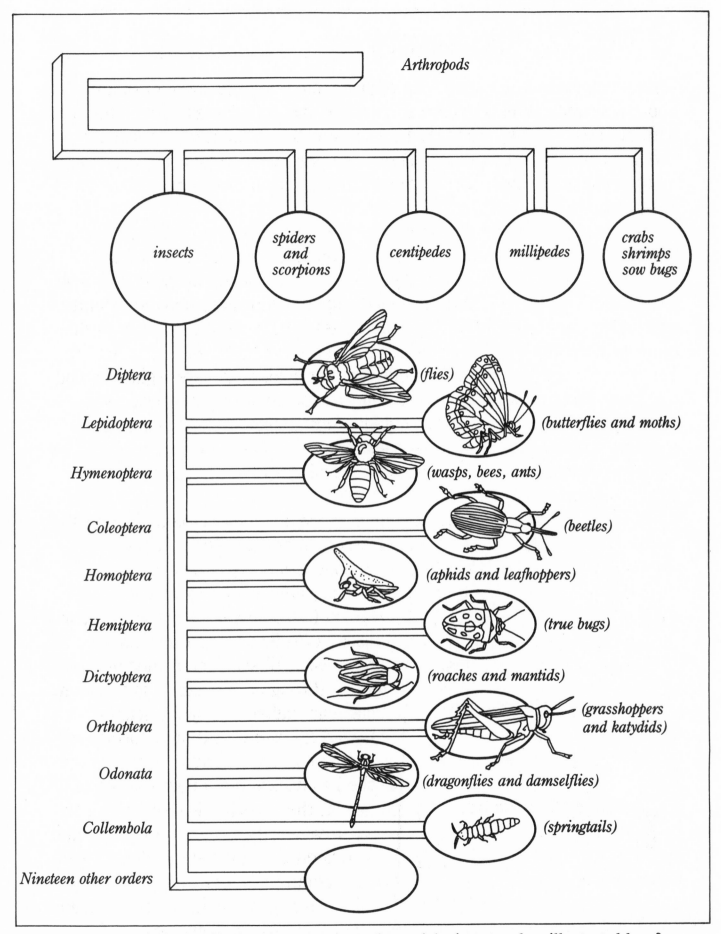

Arthropods

insects

spiders and scorpions

centipedes

millipedes

crabs shrimps sow bugs

Diptera *(flies)*

Lepidoptera *(butterflies and moths)*

Hymenoptera *(wasps, bees, ants)*

Coleoptera *(beetles)*

Homoptera *(aphids and leafhoppers)*

Hemiptera *(true bugs)*

Dictyoptera *(roaches and mantids)*

Orthoptera *(grasshoppers and katydids)*

Odonata *(dragonflies and damselflies)*

Collembola *(springtails)*

Nineteen other orders

The arthropod ''family tree''—have you seen members of the insect orders illustrated here?

Building a Bug

Here's a challenge: design a tough, strong creature that can eat, breathe, run, fly, reproduce, and receive information about the world around it. Insects can do all these things and more. Let's see how they do it by building an insect piece by piece.

All insects have three main body sections: a *head,* an *abdomen,* and a *thorax.* These three parts form the insect body's frame. While mammals, birds, fish, and reptiles have their skeletons on the insides of their bodies, insects have skeletons on their outsides. The insect skeleton is called the *exoskeleton.* It's made of a hard material known as *chitin* (KI-tin). This shell protects the soft interior organs and supports the body. The head, thorax, and abdomen will be joined together with flexible joints that will allow your insect to move.

Now for the head. Place eyes on your insect's head to help it find food and watch for trouble. But insects don't rely on sight alone. Equip each side of your insect's forehead with an antenna. Antennae are flexible organs loaded with sensors. They'll allow your insect to taste, smell, and detect heat.

Once your insect finds food, it must eat. The shape of its mouth will depend on what kind of food it will eat. Grasshoppers, for example, have a large set of cutting plates called *mandibles* that help them cut and chew plants. The long tongues of butterflies are perfect for sipping nectar. And the large jaws of hunting insects are engineered for seizing and killing prey.

You'll want your insect to move around. Every insect has six jointed legs attached to its thorax. Some insect legs are designed for swimming, some for jumping, and some for clinging to plants. While all insects have legs, only some have wings. Wings require strong muscles to make them move. Wings are always anchored to the thorax, too.

You should place your insect's stomach and intestine in the abdomen. These organs digest food and provide your insect with energy. On the sides of the abdomen are small holes called *spiracles* (SPIR-ih-kuhls). Fresh air is drawn through the spiracles into a series of air sacs. These are your insect's lungs. Old air is pumped out the rear spiracles.

All insects have these basic parts in common. But the sizes, shapes, and colors of insects are wildly different. Nature has designed insects that can live almost anywhere and do just about anything.

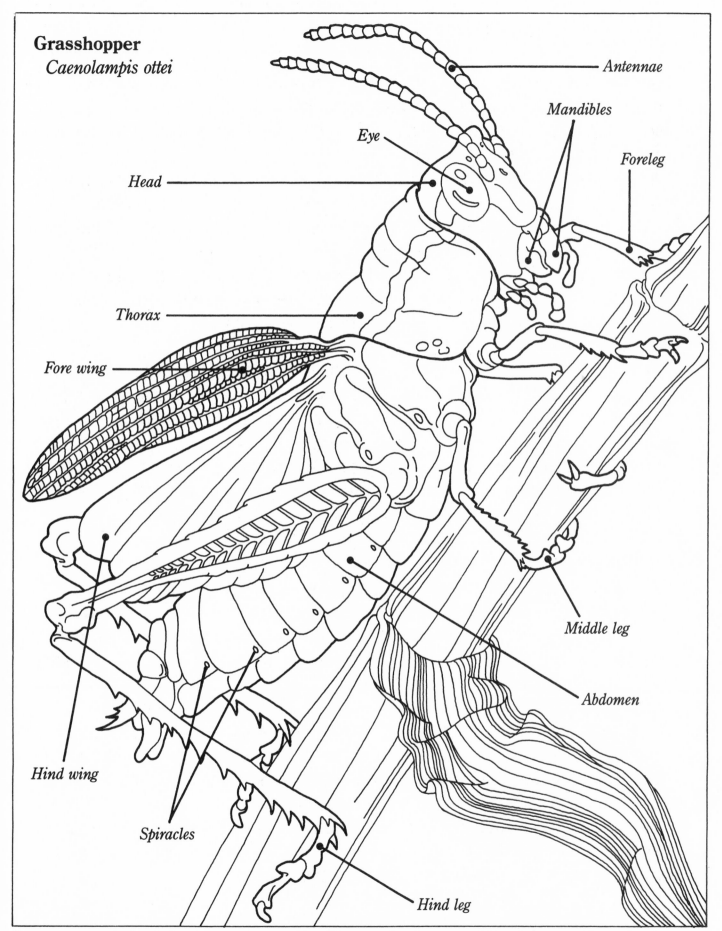

Grasshopper
Caenolampis ottei

Antennae

Mandibles

Foreleg

Eye

Head

Thorax

Fore wing

Middle leg

Abdomen

Hind wing

Spiracles

Hind leg

Insects wear their skeletons on the outside, like a suit of armor. Like the parts of a suit of armor, the parts of an insect's body are attached with flexible joints.

Buggy Eyes

Staring face to face with a horsefly means staring into a pair of eyes. Most of a horsefly's face is taken up by its rainbow-colored eyes. Horseflies need good vision to locate food. Their huge eyes are designed to function in bright light. To help cut glare, the eyes are coated with a sun screen that makes the surface reflect the bright green, yellow, and purple.

Known as *compound eyes,* insect eyes are hard and rigid structures made of many tiny *facets* (FAS-its). A facet is a tiny lens that lets light into the eye. Each facet captures a narrow view of the insect's surroundings. Insect brains then combine all these pictures. This allows insects to see the world around them.

The more facets an insect eye has, the better the insect can see. Many ants have only nine to 300 facets in each eye. (Ants rely more on their sense of smell.) Those master hunters, the dragonflies, have globe-like eyes that contain 28,000 facets of various sizes.

Humans (and other mammals) can focus their eyes. We can look at objects close up and then focus on objects far away. But the lenses in insect eyes are fixed and cannot change focus. This means that insects can see well only in a certain range, usually 50 feet or less.

Though insect eyes are not as flexible as ours, they have greater sensitivity to light and colors. The eyes of bees, butterflies, and flies are especially sensitive to color, which helps these insects find flowers. Insects can also see ultraviolet light, which is invisible to humans. Many flowers and insects have markings which are visible in ultraviolet light. We can't see these marks with our eyes, but insects can. These markings are designed to attract insects to flowers or to each other.

An added advantage of insect vision is the ability to see polarized light beams. These are unreflected beams of light from the sun. Humans can only see reflected light, which is light that has bounced off an object. Insects can detect the straight beams of light coming from the sun even on cloudy days. Bees can use the sun as a direction-finder and use it to navigate to new flower beds, even when the sun is hidden.

Vision is critical to the survival of insects because it allows them to locate food, find mates, detect danger, and navigate through their world.

With its many-lensed eyes, here's how an insect might see a toad.

First in Flight

When the Wright brothers launched their plane from the dunes of Kitty Hawk, North Carolina in 1903, humans began their conquest of the air. But before humans, birds, or even the ancient flying reptiles took to the air, the insects were buzzing above the ground.

In fact, the first fliers were insects that appeared 300 million years ago—150 million years before *Archaeopteryx,* the first bird-like creature. The early fliers included dragonflies with wingspans as long as 30 inches (76 centimeters). These giants skimmed ponds and alighted on giant tree ferns and horsetail plants. At the same time, other winged insects such as roaches and mayflies also flourished.

The insects you see in your yard are the result of millions of years of evolution and can perform amazing feats. The common hover fly, for example, has incredible flying speed and agility. It darts, hovers, and even flies backwards.

How do they do it? The wings of dragonflies are powered by muscles attached directly to the base of the thorax. These muscles make the wings beat 30 to 40 times a second—so fast you can't really see them. Dragonflies can cruise at 18 miles per hour (29 kilometers per hour) and cover great distances nonstop. The flight muscles of bees and flies are attached to the top and bottom of the thorax. Since their wings are short, bees and flies must move their wings very quickly in order to stay in the air. Flies beat their wings between 100 and 200 times per second.

All this flying makes these insects terribly hungry. They must continually provide themselves with energy. Bees can run out of energy within 15 minutes. They must stop and eat often. Busy bees and flies must regularly visit flowers for nectar.

For insects, flight is a way to escape enemies, find food, and locate mates. Nine out of ten insect species have the ability to fly during some stage of their lives. Even though we have planes and helicopters, insect flight continues to fascinate us. Aerospace engineers have studied dragonflies in wind tunnels to discover their secrets. But even with computers and high technology, we have yet to fully understand how bees buzz through the air.

The dragonfly, bumblebee, and paper wasp (rear) and cockchafer beetle (front) knew how to fly long before people did.

From Flying Goliaths to Invisible Fairies

Insects come in a wide range of sizes, from large moths to microscopic beetles. We think of insects as small creatures, so it's a surprise to encounter a large insect. One of the biggest is the giant longhorn beetle of South America. It's six inches (13 centimeters) long and has powerful jaws. The black and white Goliath beetle of Africa reaches five inches (12.5 centimeters) in length. Despite its great size, it's able to fly above the trees of the rain forests.

Still, these creatures are not very big when compared to other animals. Why don't insects grow larger? The reason is found in the exoskeleton. The material that makes up insect skeletons can withstand only a certain amount of stress before it buckles. Insects can't be larger because their exoskeletons wouldn't be able to withstand the weight. If the Goliath beetle were larger, it would lose its ability to fly because its wings could not lift it.

Insects have found success being small, and even microscopic. The fairy fly is a wasp with feather-like wings. Only 1/20 of an inch (one millimeter) in length, these wasps dive into water to lay eggs on the eggs of diving beetles. The smallest known insects are dwarf beetles that nibble on fungus. They're as little as 1/88 of an inch (1/4 of a millimeter) long.

Being small has its advantages. Tiny insects need less food, less time to hatch and grow, and can easily hide from predators. They are able to live almost anywhere—from the linings of books to the stems of flowers.

The giant longhorn beetle in this picture is shown life-size. You'd need a powerful magnifier to see the tiny fairy fly next to it.

Shedding Suits

When growing, all insects shed their skins and change their shapes many times. These stages and dramatic changes separate insects into two groups.

Several kinds of insects hatch from eggs as *nymphs*. Nymphs look much like their parents. As they shed their skins, or molt, nymphs develop larger wings and acquire the colors and patterns of their parents. After four to eight molts, nymphs become mature adults and can breed. This type of gradual growth is called *incomplete metamorphosis* (MET-uh-MOR-fuh-sis). Metamorphosis means "to change." Termites, grasshoppers, roaches, leafhoppers, cicadas, and earwigs undergo incomplete metamorphosis to reach adulthood.

Many water-born species undergo a similar but dramatic change from a swimming nymph to a flying adult. Mayfly nymphs have feather-like tails for swimming and breathe underwater through gills. The nymphs look completely different from the adults. When they reach the second to last molt, the nymphs float to the surface on a golden bubble of gas that develops in their wing case. When the nymph touches the surface, the old skin splits and a fragile mayfly pulls itself out. Then it leaves its watery nursery and flies to the nearest shrub or branch.

At this stage, the adult mayflies are easy targets for bats, fish, swallows, and dragonflies. Once on shore, mayflies shed their skins once more and become mature adults with clear, strong wings. They only live a short time, which they spend searching for a mate and laying eggs.

Other insects go through a more complex form of metamorphosis. You can read about it in the next section.

Mayfly eggs and nymphs grow and develop in a watery world. The adults spend their brief lives on land and in the air.

Magical Metamorphosis

Have you ever watched a butterfly emerge from its chrysalis, spread its wings, and fly away? This miraculous change from a caterpillar to a beautiful winged insect is called *complete metamorphosis*. Insects such as moths, butterflies, flies, wasps, and beetles undergo this dramatic transformation from egg to adulthood by way of a resting stage called a *pupa* (PYU-puh).

For example, a black swallowtail butterfly's life begins as a small egg on a parsley or carrot leaf. Within a week, a tiny *larva* hatches. Most people call butterfly larvae *caterpillars*. The larva's job is to eat and eat and grow and eat. As it grows, it sheds its skin several times. By the third shedding the caterpillar has bold green and black bands with yellow spots.

When the caterpillar has completed its fourth shedding, it stops eating and goes in search of a solid stem. On the stem it spins a silken pad. The caterpillar locks its hind feet onto the pad and then runs a thin thread around its upper body and the stem. This thread looks much like the harness that a telephone repair worker uses to hold himself or herself to telephone poles.

With its head up, the caterpillar starts wiggling out of its skin. The butterfly is now a pupa. During the pupal stage, the body of the caterpillar undergoes a complete change. After ten to 12 days, the skin of the pupa splits and the butterfly squirms free. Its crinkled, soft wings are folded. As the swallowtail hangs from the broken chrysalis, blood from its body pumps into the wings, filling and stretching them. The adult insect is very vulnerable at this time because it is unable to escape predators.

Once its wings are fully expanded, the swallowtail withdraws the fluid from the veins and the wings harden. The butterfly will test the large black, yellow, and blue-spotted wings and then fly in search of nectar.

CHRYSALIS OR COCOON?

All insects that undergo complete metamorphosis pass through the pupal stage. Some pupae have been given names. A butterfly pupa is called a chrysalis. *Every chrysalis has a hard shell and is camouflaged by color and shape to match foliage or bark. A moth pupa is usually encased in a silken envelope called a* cocoon. *Made from fine threads of silk, cocoons protect moth pupae from weather and wasps.*

cocoon

chrysalis

The caterpillar, pupa, and adult of the eastern black swallowtail butterfly look very different from one another.

Six-legged Cows

In the summer, you may drive by lush farms and fields and see cows placidly munching away on grasses. These huge animals often keep the meadows mown to the ground. Hidden from view are a host of much smaller six-legged "cows" eating the same greenery.

To see these creatures, take a walk in a field and watch the green and yellow grasshoppers jump away from your feet. A cow (3,000 pounds, or 1,350 kilograms) weighs 460,000 times as much as a grasshopper (1/10 of an ounce, or three grams). But in great numbers, grasshoppers are able to consume tremendous amounts of grass.

In the western United States, huge numbers of grasshoppers have destroyed crops as they've traveled by wing in search of food. Such plagues were one of the hazards farmers had to endure before pesticides became available.

So common was one species of grasshoppers that they have made a Montana glacier famous. During the late summer, when the glacier melts, large numbers of frozen grasshoppers fall to its base. Entomologists have identified these dead grasshoppers as an extinct species that was frozen in the glacier thousands of years ago. After the discovery of these insects, the glacier was called Grasshopper Glacier.

How did these thousands upon thousands of grasshoppers become trapped in the ice? Scientists have suggested that a large swarm flew over the glacier during poor weather and was forced to land on the ice. Unlike humans, cows, and other mammals which generate their own body heat, insects need an external source of heat to survive in cool weather. Unable to stay warm, the insects could not leave the glacier and became entombed in the ice.

Like all insects, grasshoppers are unable to generate heat for their bodies. They use the sun to help warm their bodies and digest the tough plant fibers in their stomachs. When the weather is warm, these insects continue eating into the night. When the temperature is too hot they seek shade.

A lack of warmth is what trapped the grasshoppers of Grasshopper Glacier.

Cows are not the only animals chewing their cuds in the meadows. Grasshoppers and cows compete for the same grass.

Micro-Miners

To obtain salt, gold, diamonds, copper, coal, and other important resources, our miners dig deep into the earth. However, humans are not the only miners on earth. For millions of years, insects have been carving out tunnels in the ground—and also in plants.

Perhaps the best known miners are ants. Some species dig tunnels up to 30 feet (nine meters) deep. Some observant gold hunters have found chips of ore brought to the surfaces by deep-digging ants. Ants excavate tunnels to create safe places to raise their young and survive periods of extreme heat, drought, and cold. Leafcutter ants of the rain forests in South America dig and build large nests complete with underground fungus gardens and ventilation shafts. These nests can hold a million workers.

Other micro-miners specialize in digging tunnels in trees and even in thin leaves. The larvae of painted borers and long-horn beetles chew tunnels under bark and through the hard trunks of trees. Some varieties can be heard in old logs as they munch away.

Some of the tiniest miners make networks of tunnels in leaves. Certain species of tiny beetles, flies, and feather-winged moths lay eggs on leaves. The larvae eat away patterns in the narrow space between the top and bottom surfaces of the leaves. Each species creates its own unique pattern.

Look for micro-miners in the leaves of trees and in fallen wood. Peel back the bark of a fallen tree and you'll find the mazes created by bark beetles and other tunnelers.

bark
beetles

leaf
cutter
ants

leaf miner
fly larvae

Micro-miners break down decaying wood and help make the soil suitable for plant growth.

Seventeen Years to Wait

Every 17 years a plague returns to the eastern United States. Newspapers print stories warning of the arrival of hundreds of thousands of strange creatures. Anticipating the appearance of these hordes of noisy animals, people leave their homes for the summer.

What are these animals? They are 17-year cicadas. These red-eyed and black-bodied insects infest neighborhoods during the month of June.

The lives of these amazing insects start as eggs embedded in the twigs of trees. The eggs hatch and the larvae immediately burrow into the ground and sink their tubular mouths into plant roots. For 17 long years, the cicada larvae drink sugars from roots. During this time they gradually grow, shedding their skins several times until they become an inch (two and one-half centimeters) long.

During their seventeenth summer, the larvae claw their way to the surface and climb any nearby objects: trees, walls, twigs, and trellises. Once they get a yard above the ground, they stop and anchor themselves. Their skins split and winged adults struggle free from the brown cases.

The next day the cicadas climb higher and test their wings. The males move high into the trees and begin generating a loud, obnoxious buzz to attract mates. Some species produce sounds that can be heard more than a mile away. Hundreds of male 17-year cicadas may be concentrated in one area—and this can produce a deafening din.

To make these sounds, cicadas have a pair of plate-like structures called *tymbals* at the base of their abdomens. Muscles flex these plates, which causes them to create a series of clicks. The muscles work so quickly that the clicks turn into a loud buzz.

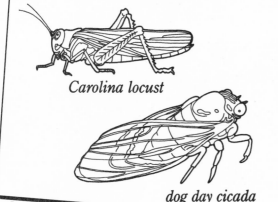

LOCUST OR CICADA?

Do you know the difference? Most people call buzzing insects locusts. But these loud creatures are properly known as cicadas. True locusts are grasshoppers that migrate in large swarms. They cannot make loud noises.

Carolina locust

dog day cicada

Buzzzzz! After a long stay underground, this adult cicada leaves behind its old brown pupal skin.

Terrible Tigers

Did you know that tigers live in almost every part of the world? Some are probably near your favorite beach, on your baseball field, and in your neighborhood. With large eyes, menacing jaws, and long legs, these *carnivores* (CAR-nuh-VORS), or meat-eaters, quickly chase down their prey. Fortunately for us, they're less than an inch (two and one-half centimeters) long.

These hunters are tiger beetles. Often bright green with white spots, they prowl sunny paths and sandy barrens in search of insects to eat. Usually, they scurry from human feet and take wing when threatened.

More than 1,500 species of tiger beetles inhabit the earth. The greatest number are found near the equator. Not all are found during the day. The largest, called the night hunter, stalks the African grasslands. Another nocturnal (active at night) tiger beetle lives on the shores of the Amazon River in South America. It emerges at dusk to hunt unsuspecting insects, spiders, and whatever washes up on the banks.

All tiger beetles go through a stage in which the larvae ambush their prey. Known in the southern United States as doodlebugs, tiger beetle larvae are worm-like with hard flat heads and large jaws. They dig holes in the ground and hide at the bottom. If you slip a piece of grass into a doodlebug pit, the larva will grab ahold of it and pull with all its strength.

When not disturbed, the voracious larvae wait for unsuspecting creatures to pass. If a spider places its foot at the edge of a doodlebug hole, the hungry larva will seize the spider and pull it into the hole. The larva eventually matures within its tunnel and becomes another miniature six-legged tiger.

Fast on their feet, tiger beetles will pounce on anything that moves.

Praying for Food

Perhaps the most famous insect predators are praying mantises. These sticklike creatures make interesting pets to watch. Mantises are fearsome hunters that are camouflaged, patient, and fast.

Mantis bodies are designed for hunting. Their slim green forms blend well with grass and other plants. Their heads turn freely and feature large eyes—just as the wolf said to Little Red Riding Hood, "Better to see you, my dear."

Mantises are famous for the pair of arms beneath their heads. These are folded neatly, as if the mantises are holding them in prayer. But these arms have rows of sharp spines and are deadly weapons. Mantises hunt by sneaking up on their victims. As they approach unsuspecting insects, they sway side to side to imitate blowing twigs. While performing this motion, the mantises are carefully judging the distance to their targets. When in range, mantises lunge forward and snag their unfortunate prey.

The mating ritual of mantises is deadly, too. Male mantises are smaller than the females. After mating, the females kill and eat their mates. This sounds severe, but it's nature's way of making sure that the females have enough food to produce healthy eggs.

Mantis egg cases are hard, brown structures that look as if they are made of foam. You can find them attached to branches and twigs. Inside each case are hundreds of eggs, which burst open in the spring and produce a multitude of miniature mantises. These nymphs roam the foliage of the area, eating anything they're able to grab.

The large-mantises found in the United States came from Europe and China. So hungry and strong are these insects that adults have been seen catching small birds, such as wrens and hummingbirds, as well as lizards and frogs!

Mantises are patient hunters. When this moth lands, the mantis will snag it with its spiny arms.

Perilous Pits

Imagine standing in the desert on the edge of a pit 40 feet (12 meters) deep. The sand gives way and you slide and tumble to the bottom—kuh-wump! You shake off the grit and start climbing back to the rim. As you do, the sand gives way and slows your progress. And as you dislodge more sand, the movement awakens a monster that lies buried at the bottom of the pit.

Looking down, you see two large jaws lined with long pointed teeth lifting out of the sand below you. They grab for you. Frantically, you scramble up the side of the pit to escape this fearsome creature. But the sand keeps pouring down, and the monster showers you with more sand. Suddenly the whole side of the pit gives way and you slide down into the jaws, which pull you under, never to be seen again.

For us, this is just a scary dream. But it's no dream in the insect world. For ants, these monsters in pits really exist.

Perhaps you have noticed small quarter-sized pits in the sand under a bridge or near the edges of a building. These seemingly insignificant depressions are made by the larvae of winged insects called ant lions. Hidden at the bottom of each pit, these larvae wait for any insect that may fall into their traps. When insects (usually ants) fall in, their movements signal the larvae to surface. Ant lions expose only their heads and jaws during captures.

To gain nourishment, the larvae inject through the end of its pincers a fluid that liquifies the insides of the ants. The ant lions then use their hollow jaws as straws to drain the ants' bodies. When done, the ant lions leave the husks buried in the sand and wait for more victims.

To become adults, ant lion larvae weave themselves into silken balls covered with sand. Inside, the larvae undergo metamorphosis. Adult ant lions look much like damselflies and have two pairs of heavily veined wings. Certain species grow to five inches (12 centimeters) long and continue to hunt insects at night. Look for them at the lights around your house.

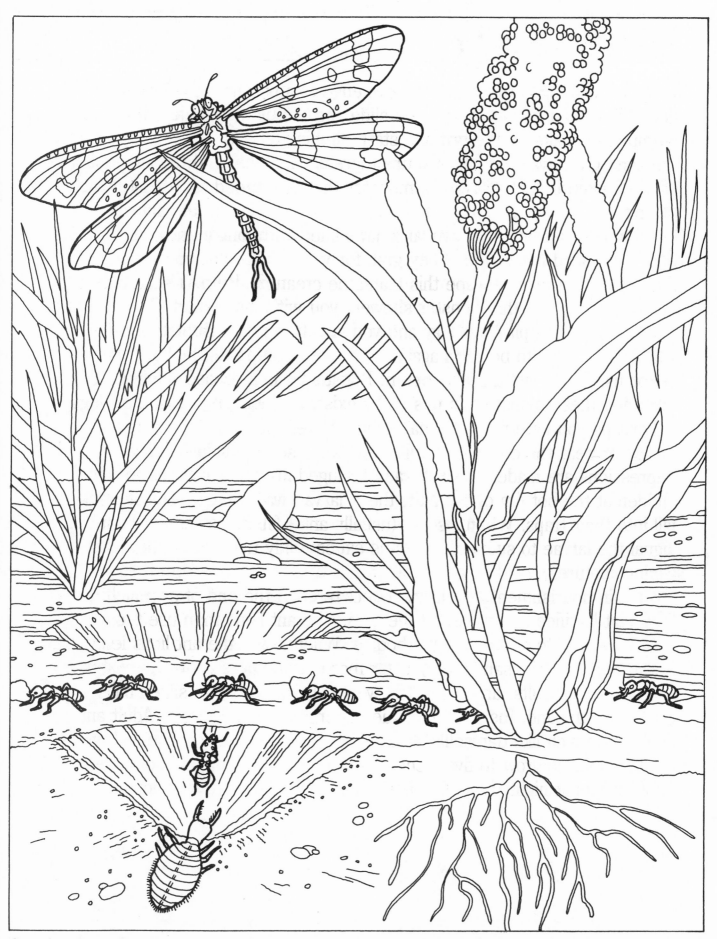

Straying from the path, an ant blunders into an ant lion's trap. Flying above is an adult ant lion.

Damsels and Flying Dragons

Their nicknames include "bee butcher," "mosquito hawk," and "spider hunter." Dragonflies and damselflies are marvelous hunters and masters of flight.

Dragonflies were the first animals to successfully take to the air—millions of years before the birds. With two pairs of glistening wings, these flying predators maintain their flight using a technique unique in the animal kingdom. Unlike flies and butterflies, which beat their wings in unison, dragonflies are able to stay aloft by alternating the strokes of each pair of their wings. When the first pair is up, the second is down. This alternating beat allows these aerial hunters to hover easily in one spot.

Usually found near bodies of water, dragonflies prefer hunting in the warmth and bright light of the sun. They perch on plants, looking for prey. When they spot tasty-looking insects, dragonflies can chase them at 20 miles (32 kilometers) per hour. Dragonflies trap their prey with their legs, which close into a deadly basket-like prison.

Damselflies are smaller-bodied relatives of the dragonflies. While dragonflies hold their wings flat, damselflies hold their wings up over their abdomens. Damselflies have blue-green bodies and clear-to-almost-black wings. In the tropics, a group of damselflies are known as spider hunters. These hunters fly among the trees in search of spider webs. Their clear wings are tipped in white and yellow to distract predators from their bodies. Some tropical damselflies have wingspans of up to seven inches (15.5 centimeters).

As larvae, dragonflies and damselflies control insect populations below the water's surface. As adults, they control insect numbers above the water.

Have you ever tried to catch a dragonfly (top and bottom) or a damselfly (middle)? Their speed and excellent eyesight make it difficult.

The Blind Legions

What do you do when your food is bigger and stronger than you? This is the problem for ants. Ants are powerful for their size, but are easily outweighed by the worms, beetles, caterpillars, and other creatures they eat. The solution is teamwork. For some species, help can come in the millions.

Worker ants cooperate to capture and collect food. Army ants cooperate in an unusual way. They overwhelm their prey with sheer numbers. One army ant colony can contain more than a million members!

In the rain forests of Central and South America, army ants move their colonies frequently, sometimes every day. Rather than construct nests in the ground, army ants build nests with their own bodies! These nests are called *bivouacs* (BIV-oo-aks). Bivouacs are started by workers that suspend themselves under a log or branch. Other ants grab hold. Soon, layers of interlocking ants form living walls around the queen. Since these walls are made of biting and stinging ants, bivouacs offer great protection against predators.

Each morning, the bivouac breaks up and the army ants stream into the forest in a wave ten feet (three meters) wide. As they advance across the forest floor, the ants surprise, capture, and dismember all animals in their path. Every creature that can walk, slither, hop, or fly tries to escape the ferocious jaws and potent stings of the army ants. It causes a great deal of noise and confusion. If you stood near a wave of these ants, you could hear the rustling of leaves and the calls of alarmed animals.

Captured prey is killed and taken to the bivouac at the end of the day to feed the ants and their larvae. The column is guarded by large-jawed, blind soldier ants. Army ants seldom kill large animals, which can escape them easily.

In Brazil, army ants sometimes invade a house or farm. For a few hours or a day, the house must be left to the ants. It's a nuisance, but the ants do provide a helpful service. The ants drive insects, lizards, mice, scorpions, and snakes out of the house. Then the column moves on, leaving the house free of pests. The army ants are the forest's exterminators.

With their strong jaws and painful stings, a squad of army ants mobs a katydid that couldn't get away.

The Pollinators

Every day we benefit from the gifts of flowering plants. Peaches, apples and oranges fill our fruit bowls, while orchids, daisies, and lilies grace our tables. The wide variety of flowers and fruits we enjoy is made possible by insects.

To produce seeds, most plants must receive pollen from another plant of the same species. Pollen fertilizes the seeds of plants. Some plants depend on the wind to carry their pollen grains. But other plants take advantage of a more reliable way of bringing together pollen grains and unfertilized seeds: insects.

Six-legged creatures are highly efficient at transferring pollen from one plant to the next. To attract insects to pick up pollen, many plants present attractive flowers that offer sweet rewards. Lured by nectar, bright colors, and fragrant scents, insects have become the delivery service for plant reproduction. After millions of years, the plant-insect relationship has created a rich variety of flowers—and many insects pollinate only certain flowers.

The master pollinators are the bees. The first buzzes you hear in the spring come from bumblebees. Blooming in late May, pink ladyslipper orchids depend on bumblebees. Getting inside these flowers is difficult for most insects, but brawny bumblebees can squeeze into the flowers and pollinate them.

In the island country of Madagascar, the Star of Bethlehem orchid produces a large five-pointed flower that has a six-inch-long (18 centimeter) nectar tube. Such a long nectar tube needs a special insect pollinator to reach the nectar. For years, no one knew what visited this large orchid until one night a small gray sphinx moth was captured. This night flyer had a tongue three times the length of its body! Without this insect, the Star of Bethlehem would become extinct.

Some flowers are shaped to deceive insects. In Europe, the wasp orchid imitates a local wasp's shape and emits an odor that mimics the odor of the female wasp. This orchid fools male wasps into landing on the flowers and pollinating them.

When this bumblebee lands on flowers, pollen grains stick to its fuzzy legs and body.

Bees Are Big Business

The best known pollinators are honeybees. Bees live in large colonies called *hives*. Within the hives, bees are divided into three classes: workers, drones, and queens. The workers build the hives, find food, and defend the colony. The drones eat and wait until they are called to mate with the queen. Each hive has one queen. The queen is the focus of hive activity because she produces the eggs from which more bees hatch.

Humans have had a long relationship with bees. Before people discovered how to refine sugar, honey was the major source of sweetener. Today, honeybees are an essential part of our agriculture.

Millions of years of evolution have adapted honeybees to pollinate flowers. With their long tongues, they can sip nectar from a variety of plants. Collected nectar is converted into honey, which is the food of the colony. On their hind legs, bees have structures called *pollen baskets*. Honeybees collect pollen and stuff it into their pollen baskets. Back at the hive, the pollen is converted into a nutritious food called *beebread,* which is fed to the larvae.

Honeybees are far more valuable as pollinators than as producers of honey. In California, trucks travel at night to deliver hives of resting bees to large orchards. Farmers rent the bees to pollinate their fruit trees. Some experts estimate that the value of honeybees to our production of fruits and vegetables is about $9 billion! Without these insects, our grocers' shelves would be empty of many of our favorite fruits.

BEE DANCES

Honeybees communicate complex messages by dancing! To direct other workers to a rich source of nectar, a honeybee starts a dance by walking a straight line. As she walks she wags her tail and buzzes. At the end of the line she turns and walks in a semicircle back to the start of the line.

The length and direction of the straight line tells the other bees the distance and direction to the nectar source. The noise made by the dancing bee communicates the quality and quantity of flowers. A very noisy bee tells of a plentiful source of food. During the dance, the other bees receive samples of the nectar from the dancing bee. This helps the bees identify the flowers.

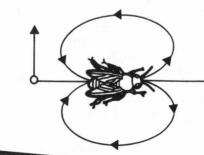

Honeybees are probably the most useful insects to humans. Most of the trees that give us fruit are pollinated by bees.

The Cleanup Crew

Everyone complains about flies buzzing around garbage. Despite our dislike for such insects, they play a critical role in nature by getting rid of dead animals, trees, and other organic waste. Insects make sure that nothing is wasted.

Have you ever wondered what happens to the bodies of deer or squirrels when they die? They seem to vanish except for a few bones. When an animal dies, it is the larvae of blow, blue bottle, green bottle, and flesh flies that break down the dead body. The larvae use the corpse as food so they can develop into adults. Black and orange sextant beetles help bury portions of the body. Dermestid and clerid beetle larvae remove the remaining pieces from the skeleton. With the combined effort of vultures, insects, and bacteria, an entire horse carcass in the jungle can be reduced to bones in less than five days. This clean-up service is reliable and fast.

Not only are dead animals eaten and buried—decaying plant materials are, too. Decomposing trees attract a multitude of insects. Long-horned beetles lay their eggs in the dead limbs of trees. Their larvae, along with those of black bessy bugs, help break down fallen trees and stumps.

Humans produce more waste and garbage than any other animal on the planet. We should appreciate the superb services that insects provide to keep the environment clean.

Among the fallen twigs and leaves on the ground, a greenbottle fly and two carrion beetles search for dead animals.

Pesky Parasites

To survive, many insects prey on other insects. Dragonflies eat flies, and ant lions trap ants. Some insects have found it better to feed by living on or within the bodies of other insects. These freeloaders are called *parasites*. Parasites need specific animals, called *hosts*, to complete their life cycles. Parasites are bad for their hosts and usually kill them.

The group containing wasps, bees, and ants contains a tremendous number of parasites. Of the 250,000 wasp species, about half parasitize other living organisms, from trees to caterpillars.

Ichneumon (ik-NYOO-men) wasps are prominent parasites. Their hosts are the larvae of woodboring horntail wood wasps. With their black and white antennae quivering, female ichneumon wasps search tree trunks for telltale odors of wood wasp larvae. The antennae are extremely sensitive and can reliably detect the location of these hidden hosts-to-be.

Upon locating wood wasp larvae, female ichneumons raise their abdomens and position their long tails between their hind legs. The ichneumon wasps plant their jagged tails into the wood and then walk in circles. This drives their tails through the wood. After 20 to 30 minutes, they reach the larvae and the female wasps force an egg into each chamber where a wood wasp larva sits. These eggs later hatch and the ichneumon larvae eat the wood wasp larvae.

Other parasitic wasps do not have to work as hard to locate hosts. Many species lay their eggs on the caterpillars of butterflies and moths. As the caterpillars grow, the wasp larvae grow within the caterpillars. The wasp larvae eventually tunnel out of their hosts and weave a series of white cocoons. Adult wasps hatch from these cocoons and the caterpillars die.

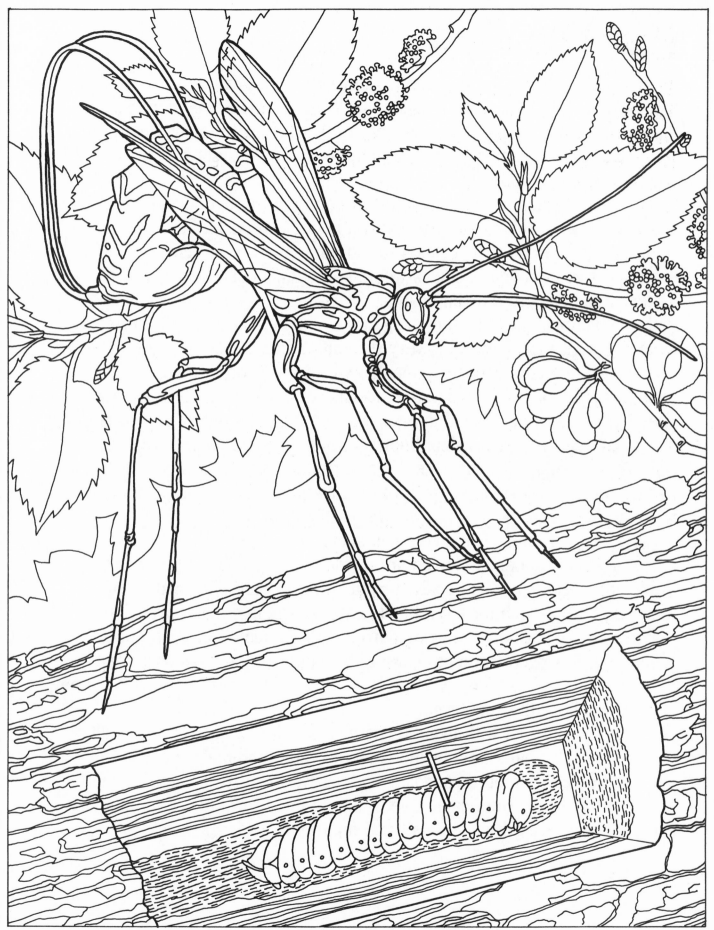

An ichneumon wasp drills through wood to lay eggs on its prey.

Dining on Wood

European explorers who traveled to Africa marveled at the great stone mounds and towers they saw rising out of the plains. Some mounds were as high as 25 feet (seven and one-half meters). Curious to know what built them, the explorers broke into the mounds and found vast numbers of what they called "white ants."

Known as termites, these insects are common throughout the warmer regions of the world and are well-known household pests. Termites make their homes in wood that touches the ground. Before the days of exterminators, wooden buildings would sometimes collapse without warning as termites hollowed out the beams.

It seems impossible that anything can eat wood. For most creatures, including plant eaters, wood is very difficult or impossible to digest. But termites have a convenient relationship with microscopic creatures called microbes. Microbes live inside the stomachs of termites. They produce chemicals that convert wood into sugars that both the microbes and termites can digest. In this relationship, known as *symbiosis* (SIM-bi-O-sis), each organism benefits from the other. The termites gain the ability to eat wood; the microbes get a steady supply of food as well as protection in the termites' stomachs.

Like ants, termites have a complex social structure that centers around a large egg-laying queen. Colonies are divided into worker and soldier groups. While ant workers are all female, termite workers are both males and females. They search for food, build nests, and help defend the colony.

When the population of a colony grows to a certain size, it produces thousands of winged termites. During the rainy season in Africa, great numbers of termites take wing and leave their home colony to establish new ones throughout the countryside.

When the skies fill with flying termites, bats, birds, and mammals all rush to eat them. Termites are nutritious food! Some mammals specialize in eating termites. Armored pangolins and aardvarks in Africa and the giant anteaters of South America all love to lap up tasty termites. Even humans capture these flying "white ants" and fry them in oil as a snack.

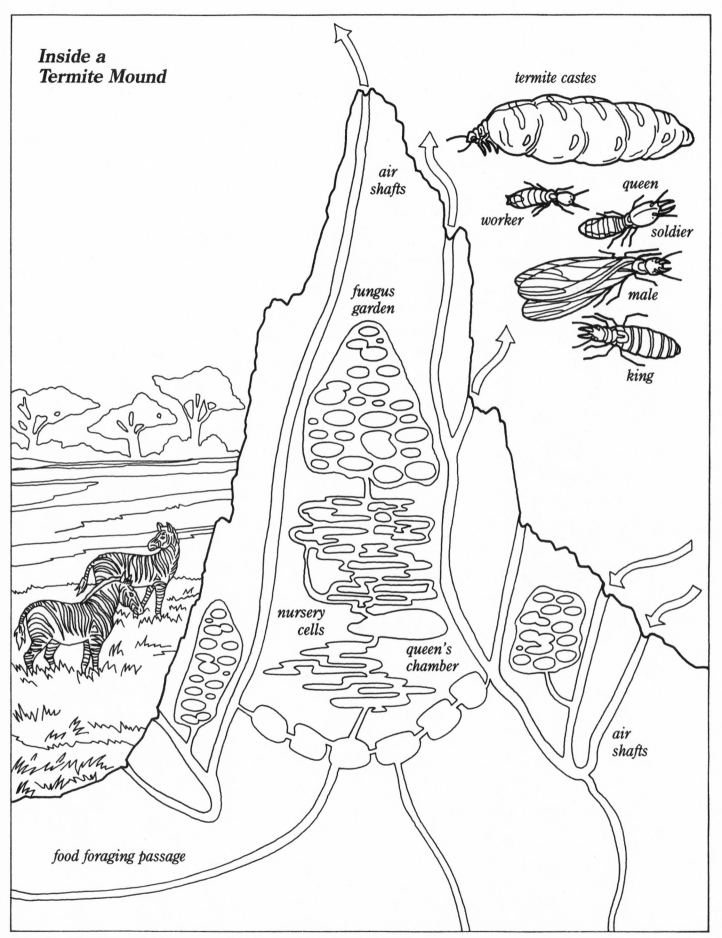

Inside a Termite Mound

termite castes

worker

queen

soldier

male

king

air shafts

fungus garden

nursery cells

queen's chamber

air shafts

food foraging passage

The inside of an African termite mound is a maze of tunnels, rooms, and air shafts.

Freeloaders

Ants spend a lot of time and energy building safe and comfortable homes. They defend their colonies from all threats, especially other ants.

But many kinds of insects are able to live inside ant nests without being molested. These insects are known as *social parasites*. They take advantage of the free food, warmth, and security they find in ant nests. Beetles, butterflies, aphids, and even spiders depend on ants and their nests for survival.

The caterpillars of European large blue butterflies start life nibbling thyme plants. But after shedding their skins three times, the caterpillars stop eating thyme. They begin producing a sweet substance from their backs. Ants love to eat this tasty stuff and carry the caterpillars back to their nests. Once there, the caterpillars eat the larvae and the eggs of the ants. The ants allow them to do this because they like the sweet liquid the caterpillars make.

Hundreds of species of beetles also successfully live with ants. To gain the trust of the aggressive ants, many kinds of beetles have the ability to produce a sweet drink from special hairs on their bodies. To further fool their landlords, some species of hister beetles are shaped—and act like—ants. To get a free meal these beetles tap the heads of ants with their antennae. This signal makes the ants give away sugar water stored in their stomachs. The beetles receive free meals from the ants just by asking.

Not all beetles are able to fool all of the ants all of the time. Sometimes they need additional defenses. Some have strange, large, flat antennae and hard, smooth shells that protect them from angry ants. Another species releases a bad odor when threatened.

What do the ants gain by having these insects sharing their nests? In most cases, nothing more than a sweet drink. The social parasites get free food and lodging.

A hister beetle (left) and the larva of a European blue butterfly (lower center) make themselves at home deep within an ant nest.

Insect Architects

The best builders in the insect world are the social insects: bees, wasps, ants, and termites. To ensure that their colonies are well-protected, these creatures build complex homes. Each species has its own style of architecture.

Bees are famous for making wax honeycombs inside trees. The basic unit of the comb is a six-sided cell. The cells are used to protect the young bee larvae and to store honey for food. People harvest the honey stored in honeycombs. If you'd like to see a honeycomb, some health food stores sell jars of honey still in the comb.

Wasps and hornets also construct combs. Instead of using wax, wasps create their construction material by grinding wood fiber in their jaws and mixing it with their saliva. This produces a paper-like substance that can be molded and formed into walls.

Using this technique, paper wasps suspend umbrella-shaped nests in trees and under the eaves of buildings. Bald-faced hornets create huge nests filled with several combs encased in layers of paper. One of the largest hornet nests was found in an attic in New Jersey. It was three feet (one meter) across.

Termites are master builders and construct a wide variety of nests throughout the warm regions of the world. Some species make underground nests, while others create tall towers. These nests are designed to capture heat. One Australian species, called the compass termite, makes a flat mound pointing north and south. This allows the mound to catch sunlight in the morning and evening. When the sun is straight overhead at noontime, little sunlight falls on the nest and this keeps it from overheating.

Just as we build homes to shield us from rain, snow, cold, and heat, insects make shelters to protect themselves from the effects of the environment.

Yellowjacket wasps build their homes layer by layer. These nests only last for a year.

Courting with Color

A large yellow sulphur butterfly flies up the river in search of a meal, a drink, or a mate. With this sulphur is a cloud of other species of yellow butterflies. To us, all these butterflies look alike. How do they tell each other apart?

To our eyes, all sulphur butterflies seem to be about the same color. But butterflies can see a kind of light, called *ultraviolet light,* that our eyes can't detect. When seen in the ultraviolet, many butterflies have bold patterns on their wings. These patterns help butterflies tell each other apart.

Color is important for insects attracting mates. Nature's rule is that the healthiest-looking mate is the best choice. Often males display the brightest colors, while females carry less striking patterns and hues. The darker colors help protect the females from predators so they can lay their eggs. When an insect species has males and females that do not look alike, the species is called *dimorphic* (dy-MOR-fik), or having two forms.

COLOR THAT NEVER FADES

The shimmering blues of morpho butterflies, the electric greens of tiger beetles, and the brilliant colors of some other insects never fade. On the wings of morphos are transparent scales that act as prisms. The scales bend incoming light and emit blue light. The bodies of other insects reflect light in similar ways, creating beautiful rainbow-like colors.

Striking examples of dimorphic insects are the morpho butterflies of Central and South America. The electric blue males flutter up and down streams. Their yellow and brown female counterparts lead a less active life in an effort to escape detection by birds.

The female morpho butterfly (bottom) has patterns of yellow and brown on its wings. In contrast, the male morpho (top) is bright blue.

Night Perfume

Large luna moths are beautiful insects of the summer months. Their pale green wings and long tails seem to glow in the moonlight. Luna moths are members of the giant silk moth family, which has some of the largest moths in the world. Like their relatives the cecropia and polyphemus moths, adult luna moths live only a week or two. During that brief time the moths must find partners, mate, and lay the eggs of the next generation.

Perhaps the most difficult part of their short existence is locating a mate. Finding a male or female by sight can be difficult at night. To increase the odds of finding each other, luna moths have a perfume that draws the males to the females.

After hatching, the female luna moths release a *pheromone* (FAIR-uh-MONE), a chemical that sends signals through smell. This chemical attracts male moths with uncanny reliability and accuracy. Males use their large feathery antennae to detect and track the females' perfume from a mile (one and one-half kilometers) or more away. The females need only to wait for their suitors to come flying by. After the male and female meet and mate, the female flies to a tree such as a maple or sweet gum and deposits her eggs on the leaves.

Both moths and butterflies produce pheromones through special scales on their wings and bodies. The colors and locations of these scales varies from species to species. On male hairstreak butterflies, dark scent spots are found on the fore wings. Male monarch butterflies have scent spots in the middles of their hind wings. Tropical swallowtail butterflies have folds in their hind wings that are filled with snowy white scent scales. When these scales are displayed during courtship, they stand out against the swallowtails' velvet black wings. As the butterflies fly, their wings rub the scales and their perfume floats into the air.

Almost all insects use pheromones to communicate to members of the same species. These scents help them attract mates, ward off enemies, and prepare each other for battle. For moths that live in a world of little light, the scent of the female ensures the continuation of each generation.

Beautiful green luna moths (top), Io moths (right), and Polyphemus moths (front, laying eggs) all use scents to attract mates.

Flashing Lights

Have you ever created a firefly lantern? On a warm summer night, get a jar, poke holes in the lid, and collect fireflies as they dance through the air. With enough of them in your jar, you can fill your bedroom with an eerie, pale green light.

During your hunt for these living lights, take time to enjoy the sight of these blinking beetles, which can cover a tree or meadow as if it's been decorated for Christmas. These insects are busy advertising for mates. Each species of firefly has its own code of blinks and flashes. Some blink at a slow steady pulse (blip...blip...blip) while others flash more rapidly (blip, blip, blip...blip, blip, blip).

Each signal is designed to locate and identify males and females of the same species. By flashing the lights in their abdomens, males signal for mates as they fly above the grass or sit on the tops of plants. The females, many of which are wingless, blink their signals from the ground. The males can easily recognize the correct signal. Once they see matching signals, the males descend to make contact with their prospective mates.

The natural light that fireflies make is called *bioluminescence* (BI-oh-LOO-meh-NES-sens). Fireflies produce a chemical that creates light without creating heat. Though scientists understand the chemical that produces the light, the ability of fireflies to turn their lights on and off is poorly understood.

Fireflies are only some of the insects with the ability to produce light. A species of fly found in the caves of New Zealand has larvae that produces light to attract insects to their sticky webs. In South America, large click beetles fly through the jungle at night with bright taillights and two headlights. Both fireflies and click beetles have light-producing larvae called *glowworms*.

After you have spent a night with your fireflies, release them the next morning so they can have a chance to find mates in the evening.

Every summer, fireflies light up the nights with their signals.

Evening Serenades

Summer nights are filled with the sounds of insects singing to their mates. These noisy insects include katydids, tree crickets, and field crickets. This group of insects employs noise-making mechanisms found near the base of their wings. For katydids, the left wing has a row of tiny hardened teeth called the *file*. The right wing has a stiffened edge called the *scraper*. The scraper is dragged rapidly over the file to produce sound. This action is similar to running your thumbnail over the teeth of a comb. With each short stroke of the wings, the scraper clicks rapidly over the 20 to 2,000 teeth of the file and in the process produces a screech. By varying the speed and movement of the wings, each species can create its own song.

Insect songs are designed to attract females. Every female is specifically tuned to the song of its species. Females become interested in singing males when the males generate the correct pitch. While most cricket chirps are within our hearing range, katydids can produce sounds far above what our ears can detect. We cannot hear them, but other katydids can.

While it's important for these insects to signal their mates, they also risk being found by predators listening for dinner. At night, bats and owls patrol the skies and trees searching for insects. Screech owls locate katydids by following their sounds. South American bats can detect singing insects—and a few species are even able to catch frogs that sing from trees!

To avoid detection, katydids and crickets devise different songs to deceive or bore predators. Some species of katydids produce a short burst of song for a second or two and then remain silent for a minute. The period of silence frustrates predators trying to track the song. Crickets throw their voices, making their songs sound as if they are coming from somewhere else. To project their chirps, they generate two pitches and even try to bounce their songs off walls or from the hollows of logs.

Try to locate a cricket or katydid at night by song alone. You'll find that it's very difficult even when the animal is singing within arm's length.

The night air is full of raspy katydid calls.

Dancing Hoppers

Many species of insects have evolved songs and even dances for courtship. To impress mates, some insects use combinations of motion, color, and sound. Such is the case for the *Syrbula* grasshoppers of Texas.

These grasshoppers locate each other using sound. They signal by rubbing their legs on their bodies. Called *stridulating*, this action generates raspy clicks. Upon hearing a female, a male tracks the noise until he finds her. If the female is ready to mate, the courtship is short, but if she isn't interested, a show begins.

To change her mind, the male grasshopper positions himself alongside the female, drops his nearest antenna in front of her, and waves it. As the antenna waves up and down, his rear legs begin stridulating. He also rocks forward and backward. Then he kicks out his feet.

As the display continues, his outer antenna waves back and forth while the inner antenna continues to move up and down. For the finale, he flashes his wings over her head several times. The whole show can last 30 minutes.

If the dance is successful, the grasshoppers will mate. But if it doesn't work, the female may reject the male with a swift kick.

Such dances are important for insects because it allows the females and males to select suitable mates. Fit and vigorous insects are the best dancers and therefore the best mates.

Male Syrbula **grasshoppers try to impress females with their fancy dance steps.**

Meeting on the Wing

Driving on a warm June night with the windows down is a regular summer ritual. But as your car approaches a river, the windshield is suddenly plastered with juicy insects that block your view. You get out and start removing the bodies. The windshield is covered, the grill is clogged, and the headlights are gooey.

This mid-summer night's traffic hazard was created by a cloud of insects participating in their annual mating flight. In Michigan, huge numbers of mayflies emerge from the water for only a brief night or two of flying before they die. During the night, these primitive insects must find mates and lay their eggs, which are deposited over or into the water.

Since they live for only a day or two, mayflies must time their mating flights perfectly so that their eggs can be fertilized. To improve their chances of making contact with mates, mayflies have huge mating flights. They take place regularly during certain nights of the year. During the spring, summer, and fall, hatches of several species will occur in a regular sequence. Trout fishermen have learned the order of the hatches and prepare trout lures to match the hatches.

Other insects, such as ants, termites, caddisflies, and flies have huge flights that involve thousands of individuals. Ant swarms have been so large and dense that people have mistaken them for smoke and called the fire department. In these clouds of insects, males seek unfertilized females. Even in the poor light of dusk or twilight, males can quickly distinguish receptive females.

Though the large flights are a great way to bring males and females together, they also attract the attention of predators such as swallows, swifts, flycatchers, dragonflies, and bats. Heavy losses are expected in these mating free-for-alls, but the insects have devised ways of increasing their chances of survival. Mayfly species often hatch during dusk and dawn. By hatching at these times, these insects fly when birds are roosting and bats are inactive. Certain species of stoneflies avoid most of their enemies by hatching in January, when most insect hunters have flown south or are hibernating.

After mating flights, male ants and mayflies die. The fertilized females find suitable places to lay their eggs and raise the next generation.

During an evening mating flight, adult mayflies take to the air. Of the thousands that take part, many will be eaten by predators.

Miniature Rhinos

When someone mentions animals with horns and antlers, you might think of reindeer, rhinos, moose, and bulls. In the world of insects, it's common to find horns and antlers on beetles. Beetles can have headgear as frightening-looking as those of much larger animals.

Few species are able to use their horns as effective weapons. These long lances and spikes are usually used for attracting mates. Many times, though, these horns are a curse. They snag on plants and rocks and get in the way.

Male stag beetles have large antler-like mandibles that are almost as long as their bodies. These multi-pointed jaws don't help stag beetles capture prey. Instead, they are used in wrestling matches with other males as they compete for mates. Some of the larger stag beetles, such as giraffe stag beetles, can reach four inches (nine centimeters) in length. Their mandibles are nearly as long as their bodies!

Scarab beetles are no less impressive with their large rhino-like horns. The olive and black Hercules beetles of Central and South America have large black horns growing from their thoraxes and heads. The horn on the thorax can be twice as long as the body. Hercules beetles can reach lengths of seven inches (17 centimeters).

TINY SAMSONS

Insects can perform incredible feats of strength. A flea can leap 100 times its length in a single bound. An ant can pull ten times its weight. If this strength was given to you, you could jump two football fields and drag thousands of pounds.

Insects are able to accomplish these acts of strength because they are small. As creatures grow in size, their weights grow faster than the strength of their muscles. Large animals must have larger muscles or more muscles to perform equivalent deeds. Fortunately for us, insects are small and elephants do not leap like fleas!

A Hercules beetle (shown here life-size) lumbers through the forest with its horn pointing the way.

Bright Colors, Bad Taste

STOP! CAUTION! DANGER! These words are found on brightly-colored road signs. These are signals to us that we should be alert and avoid something hazardous to our health.

Many insects have bright colors and bold patterns on their bodies which protect them from hungry birds and other predators.

Why do these warnings work? These insects eat plants that contain terrible-tasting chemicals. The chemicals stay in their bodies and make them unpleasant to eat. Monarch butterfly caterpillars, for example, eat milkweed, a poisonous plant. The poisons stay in the monarchs, even after the caterpillars have transformed into adults. Warning colors and patterns inform predators of their prey's nasty flavor. Predators learn what is bad to eat and avoid the creatures that carry the warning colors.

Many species of tropical grasshoppers display bright bands of purple and red to deter potential predators. South American sphinx moth caterpillars exhibit bright yellow bands that are easily seen in the dim light of the tropical rain forest. But tropical butterflies have developed the widest array of bright patterns and colors to save themselves from jacamars, relatives of kingfisher birds. A popular pattern is the bold "tiger" pattern, which is a combination of orange, black, and white stripes. Longwing butterflies of Central and South America display this pattern.

Which is good to eat—all, or none? These insects all have bold warning patterns to protect them from birds, but not all are poisonous.

Disguised as Royalty

Poisonous insects often display warning colors and patterns that keep predators away. Insects that are not poisonous have evolved patterns that make them look like their poisonous cousins. This use of disguise to appear like another creature is called *mimicry*. A great number of edible insects find protection by mimicking species that taste terrible.

Famous for their long migrations, monarch butterflies arrive in the northern United States in the spring to lay eggs on milkweed. Monarchs are poisonous. Their caterpillars display distinctive warning stripes of black, yellow, and white, and the adults have orange and black warning patterns.

Monarchs are a highly visible species and fly unmolested under the protection of their warning colors and terrible taste. Their distant relatives, the viceroys, have a similar warning pattern. But viceroys are delicious to predators. When flying, the two species look alike. But close examination reveals that viceroys are smaller, and have a simpler series of dots on their forewings. To birds, these small differences aren't enough to help them tell the two varieties of butterflies apart. The viceroys are left free to fly.

Proof that the viceroy is edible can be found in its caterpillar. Feeding on willow trees, which contain no poisons, viceroy caterpillars don't display warning colors. Instead, they attempt to look like inedible objects. In the early stages of their development, these caterpillars have contrasting patterns of brown blotches and irregular white patches. This coloration makes them look like bird droppings. Birds ignore them.

Though you may be able to distinguish monarchs from viceroys after careful examination, try to identify them correctly when they are flying. You'll understand why birds avoid both rather than risk eating an unpleasant snack.

The smaller, edible viceroy butterfly (top) has the same black veins and orange patches as the monarch (bottom).

Is It a Bee?

Because of their fearsome stings, bees and wasps get a great deal of respect from animals, including humans. To make sure they're recognized, wasps and bees have evolved distinct warning colors and patterns on their bodies. The yellow or orange bands on their dark abdomens are signals that say "Don't mess with me—if you do, I'll sting you!" When we see an insect that has yellow bands around its abdomen, we know to keep away.

Many insects imitate bees and wasps as a way of protecting themselves. Various flies, moths, grasshoppers, and true bugs display bee and wasp colors and even mimic their movements.

In the gardens of North America, yellow-banded hover flies mimic yellowjacket wasps. Hairy robber flies and bee flies mimic honey bees and fuzzy bumblebees. They not only look like bees, but also sound like them as they buzz around the yard.

Around the world, many wasps sport blue bodies with blue or orange wings and have white or yellow bands on their antennae. In your back yard you may see a blue and black ctenucha moth, which displays the colors of mud dauber wasps. In the jungles where spider-hunting wasps flourish, a whole family of moths have developed narrow transparent wings, slim bodies, and long, thin antennae, all prominently marked with blues, whites, and yellows. Even their legs have ridges of blue scales that make their delicate legs look like the strong legs of wasps.

Grasshoppers also mimic the colors and patterns of wasps. In East Africa, bandwing grasshoppers are not only colored like wasps, but also act like wasps. East African wasps are active hunters that scurry over the sand nervously flicking their wings. Picking up on this behavior, bandwing grasshoppers mimic the wasps by flashing their blue underwings.

The most successful mimics are those that can look, sound, and even act like the poisonous or dangerous creatures they imitate.

All three have yellow and black bands on their bodies, but only the yellowjacket (middle) can sting. The hover fly (bottom) and bee fly (left) are harmless.

Watch the Eyes!

How many eyes does an insect have—two, four, eight, or even more? Some insects look as if they have many pairs of eyes—but only one pair works. The other eyes are clever fakes. Why do insects need imitation eyes?

Predators tend to attack the heads of their prey, since the head is the most important part of any animal's body. Butterflies and moths and other winged insects have developed eyespots, or fake eyes, on the outer edges of their wings to distract predators away from their important body parts.

Wood satyr butterflies display a line of eyespots on the hind wings. These blue and sometimes silver spots attract birds to the wood satyrs' hind wings, which easily break away and allow the butterflies to escape.

Tiny hairstreak butterflies have thin tails that trail behind the eyespots on their hind wings. These tails imitate the hairstreaks' antennae. Hairstreaks rub their hind wings up and down. By flicking their hair-like tails, the hairstreaks lure hungry birds away from their heads. The fooled birds instead attack the tips of the tails.

Some butterflies and moths use eyespots to intimidate predators. Owl butterflies have large eyespots on their hind wings that look like the eyes of an owl or monkey. Owl butterflies rest on trunks of trees by day and fly only in the twilight of dusk and dawn. If lizards or small mammals find these resting butterflies, the large eyespots may make the predators believe that they're looking at a dangerous foe.

Atlas moths have small eyespots near the tip of each wing. Below the eyespots are red lines that look like mouths. These markings make the wing tips look like snake heads. It's sometimes enough to scare birds away.

Eyespots are a proven defense for many flying insects. You may see butterflies that have small nicks in their wings where their eyespots are displayed. These insects were able to live because the eyespots fooled a bird into biting the wing areas rather than the butterfly's important parts.

Fake eyes help the owl butterfly (top), metalmark butterfly (middle), and lanternfly (bottom) survive in the rain forest.

A Forest of Insects

In the forests of the world, flocks of birds pick through the bushes and trees in search of tasty insects. Insects must hide from these fast, efficient predators. Many insects have evolved bizarre and convincing ways of looking like plants. These insects have incredible camouflages that let them blend into their environment.

Katydids are experts at imitating foliage. Some species look like new green leaves, complete with veins. Other species appear to be brown, moldy leaves. They even have holes in their wings like damaged leaves. Their colors and patterns blend perfectly into the trees.

Many species of butterflies and moths also imitate leaves. Some butterflies display colorful wings when flying, when at rest in trees they practically vanish. When not in the air, these butterflies keep their wings closed and display only their dull underwings.

If you see a twig or small branch start moving, most likely you've found a walking stick. Relatives of katydids and grasshoppers, these odd creatures quietly graze on leaves. They move slowly and are mostly active at night to avoid predators. To add to the disguise, some walking sticks are covered with small green plates that mimic moss and lichen. Other excellent imitators of sticks are inchworms, which look like brown or bright green twigs.

The most bizarre creatures that hide on plants are treehoppers. These small jumping insects have odd bodies featuring spines, barbs, hooks, and lumps. Tropical treehoppers are perhaps the strangest looking insects of all.

The plants in your yard or park may be full of camouflaged insects. Practice finding these camouflaged creatures by locating the four insects in this illustration.

Can you spot the four leaf insects hidden in this picture? They hope you can't!

Listening for Trouble

Entomologists have found an interesting rule in the insect world. If an insect has wings during its entire adult stage, it usually has a way of hearing. Some of these listening devices are very complex and are tuned to receive sounds of specific pitches, just as a radio is tuned to receive a certain range of stations. With these ears, insects use sound to detect the approach of predators.

Katydids have ears on their forelegs. These ears appear to be smooth oval pits near the knee. While crickets also have ears in their forelegs, grasshoppers have them on the sides of their abdomens above their hind legs. Mantises have sound receivers under their thoraxes.

Many species of midges and mosquitoes have feathery antennae that receive sound waves. These receivers help male mosquitoes locate the distinctive buzz of females.

For all species that fly at night, bats are a great threat. Bats use high frequency sound to locate flying insects. As bats fly, they squeak. The sound bounces off insects in the air. Bats instantly calculate the location and distance of the insects by analyzing the returning signals. With several squeaks, a bat can use its radar to track a moth, swoop down, and grab the insect in its teeth.

As a defense against such fast and efficient hunters, moths have ears that can hear bat signals. When they hear bat squeaks, moths begin flying in erratic dips, loops, and dives. By flying wildly, moths try to make bats misjudge their locations.

Like many species of butterflies, some species of moths taste terrible. These unpleasant-tasting species display colors that warn predators away. But how do moths avoid being eaten at night, when bats can't see the warning colors? To warn bats of their bad taste, tiger moths transmit high-pitched clicks. Once a bat has tried to eat a clicking tiger moth, it will remember the unpleasant experience and not try again.

Even though moths can hear bats approaching, they often get caught anyway.

Flee, Fly, or Fall

When defenses such as camouflage, mimicry, and warning colors fail to keep predators from attacking, most insects try to escape danger. Have you ever tried catching an insect? A butterfly can avoid every swing of your net and leave you spinning on your heels. Here's how insects make quick getaways.

Most insects leap out of reach. Grasshoppers are famous for jumping. With the aid of their wings, their leaps can extend for yards. The Spanish call grasshoppers "saltamontes," which means "mountain jumpers."

Perhaps the most infamous leaper is the tiny flea. Able to fit in the letter "o" of this book's print, fleas can leap up to twelve inches (26.4 centimeters)—100 times their length. If you could jump 100 times your length, one leap would carry you two football fields away! To accomplish this great feat, fleas have pads in their bodies made of a substance called *resilin*. Resilin is more efficient than rubber at storing and releasing energy. To jump, fleas push their hind legs against the pads of resilin, which suddenly expand like springs and force the legs down, propelling the fleas into the air.

Long-snouted weevils simply drop out of sight. When threatened, these tough beetles tuck in their legs and fall to the ground. Gravity takes them out of danger. If the weevils are found again on the ground, they pretend they are dead. When still, they resemble small seeds with stems.

Flies are escape artists. Common houseflies seem to be able to read your mind as you strike at them. The eyes of flies are large and sensitive to rapid movement. They can see the shadow of your flyswatter as it comes down. They can also sense the wind caused by your swatter as it moves. These warnings often give flies enough time to zip to safety.

If it finds itself in trouble, the fuzzy acorn weevil will free-fall to safety.

The Stinkers

When you see a skunk, you probably think of one thing—the stink! These familiar black and white mammals keep enemies on the run with a spray of smelly chemicals. You may be less familiar with insects that use bad odors to keep predators away.

Stinkbugs are brightly colored bugs that sip plant juices and hunt other insects. Their orange and black coloring advertises their bad taste and noxious smell. If predators ignore the warning colors and take a bite, stink bugs emit a nasty odor to stop the attack. To get an idea of this smell, carefully hold a stinkbug on the edges of its thorax behind its head and take a whiff.

Other insects such as young African roaches find security by combining their odors. While resting at night, these gray and white roaches pack closely together with their antennae bristling out. When alarmed they give off a terrible aroma.

Fat (and often flightless) pyrgamorph grasshoppers produce a bright blue foam from their thoraxes that contains a strong odor and terrible flavor that can stop any bird or mammal. Few creatures will attempt to eat these grasshoppers—and those that do don't try again.

You'd be smart to stay away from this group of smelly beetles and stinkbugs. Phew!

Exploding Insects

Many predators are not stopped by bad odors or insect bites. That's why some insects have chemical weapons and unusual ways of delivering them. These chemical weapons give the insects a chance to escape predators. Chemicals are also effective weapons against other insects because they can penetrate their exoskeletons.

The most famous system is owned by the bombardier beetles. These creatures are walking chemical bombs. When bombardiers are threatened, chemicals mix in their abdomens and explode out the tip. When these beetles blow, their attackers are sprayed with chemicals that cause great discomfort.

Some ant species can spray potent chemicals on their enemies. Some are as powerful as man-made insecticides. Disturbed wood ants turn their tails toward attackers and eject a stinging acid.

Termites have workers equipped with nozzles on their heads. These nozzle-heads spray chemicals that surprise and stun attacking insects.

Katydids and walking sticks can spray chemicals up to 14 inches (30 centimeters) away. Some varieties of katydids squirt jets of their green blood onto attackers through seams at the base of their legs. After ejecting this goo, the seams seal themselves until needed again.

This toad gets an unpleasant surprise from a bombardier beetle.

Kick, Bite, or Sting

Imagine you're a green anole lizard. You hunt for insects in your tropical rain forest. One morning, you clamber onto a palm leaf and find a strange green insect staring back at you. It has two red eyes, a sharp horn, and an orange mouth with two sharp scissor-like jaws. Covering its legs and head are spines like the thorns on a briar bush. After a moment, you leap to another leaf in search of less exciting prey.

The well-armed creature you encountered is a large katydid. It looks frightening. But because appearances alone don't scare predators always, most insects have an active defense. In the case of katydids, they'll try to ram their spiny legs into an attacker. Grasshoppers are also known to kick predators with the spines on their hind legs.

Most insects, from narrow-mouthed weevils to large-jawed beetles, will try to bite. Few insects can actually cut the skin of humans, but they can inflict pain. The bite of the katydid featured on the facing page can draw blood. Some species of bugs and water bugs can give a nasty bite if mishandled.

Wasps and bees have another weapon—the stinger. This needle-like device injects poisons into enemies or prey. Honeybees die after stinging because their poison sacs rip away from their abdomens after their stingers have been set. Bumblebees and wasps don't sacrifice themselves when delivering a sting. They're able to lance victims repeatedly.

Some people confuse bites with stings. The bites of most bees, wasps, and ants are harmless. They bite to firmly anchor themselves as they ram their stingers into their enemies. However, many tropical bees are stingless and must rely on their effective bite to defend their hives.

For most people, a single bee or wasp sting feels like an electric shock and is followed by swelling. However, people with allergies to stings have difficulty breathing and can even die from just one sting. Whether you're allergic or not, always treat bees and wasps with great respect.

If you were a lizard, would you try to eat this spiny katydid?

Desert Dwellers

On the west coast of southern Africa is one of the world's oldest and driest deserts, the Namib. The land is covered with orange, gray, and red sand piled into giant dunes. Its rocky landscape is carved by wind that rarely brings rain. The sun is terribly hot. Some areas of this desert look like the pictures sent back from the moon and Mars. Only a few species of spiders, lizards, and insects are able to exist in this harsh habitat.

The key to survival in the desert is water. Rain may come only once every ten years to the Namib, but moisture does exist in the form of sea fog blown inland. In the mornings, black darkling beetles climb the dunes to catch fog. At the tops of the dunes, they point their abdomens into the wind and let water droplets form on their bodies. The drops grow and then slide into the beetles' mouths. After capturing water, these beetles bury themselves in the sand to avoid the hot sun and hungry lizards.

Not all deserts are as dry as the Namib. The Sonoran and Mojave Deserts of the American Southwest have more plants, including the long-armed Saguaro cactuses. There, insects such as band-winged grasshoppers flourish during times of moisture. And female tarantula hawk wasps cruise the bushes and cactuses in search of spider holes.

These large blue- and orange-winged hunters must find tarantulas as food for their young. When these wasps find the larger spiders there's a tremendous fight to the death. The wasps use their stings to paralyze the tarantulas. The spiders defend themselves with their large fangs. The wasps are incredibly strong and fast and each may subdue several spiders during their lifetimes. Once a spider is paralyzed, a wasp lays a single egg on the abdomen of the tarantula and then buries the whole spider. The buried spider gives the young wasp larva a source of food as it grows.

To survive long periods without food, desert insects try to remain inactive until rains come and the plants grow. Many insects live as eggs for years until the conditions are good for finding food. One species of darkling beetle is able to live for five years without food.

Only a few kinds of insects are able to withstand the rigors of desert living. By conserving water, avoiding heat, and remaining inactive for long periods, they scrape out a living in the world's harshest habitats.

Fights between tarantulas and their archenemies, the tarantula wasps, are among the fiercest in nature.

The African Bush

In East Africa, a unique habitat called the African bush stretches from Kenya south to eastern South Africa. During the rainy season, the countryside is lush with tall grasses. But in the dry season, only tough thorn trees and dead stalks stand. The land is filled with great numbers of elephants, rhinoceros, giraffes, zebras, and wildebeest. They follow the rains and the green grass they produce. In this land of thorn trees and exotic animals, a great number of insects have relationships with the plants and animals.

Legions of insects use dung from the grazing mammals roaming the countryside. The most common of these insects are black dung beetles. Using their scraper-like forelegs, black dung beetles build balls of dung. Then they roll these balls with their hind legs to a nesting site. The female dung beetles lay eggs on the balls and cover them with soil. The larvae hatch and use the balls for food.

The ancient Egyptians marvelled at these industrious insects. They made these beetles sacred symbols of their sun god, who rolled the sun across the sky from sunrise to sunset. Members of the dung beetle family are called scarabs. Images of scarab beetles often appear on Egyptian carvings and jewelry.

In areas of the bush where many mammals roam, tsetse (TET-see) flies also flourish. These little vampires live on blood. Measuring less than half an inch (one centimeter), tsetse flies may be the most dangerous animals in Africa. They transmit sleeping sickness to humans through their bites. This disease has killed millions of people. Elephants, gazelles, zebras, and other large animals are immune to diseases carried by tsetse flies.

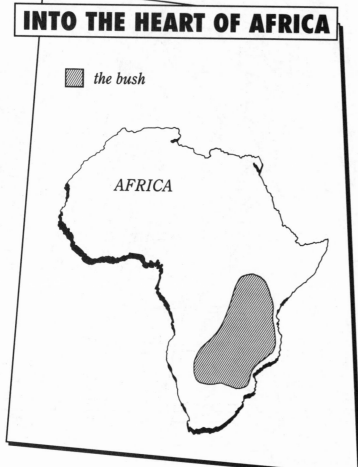

INTO THE HEART OF AFRICA

the bush

AFRICA

Under the feet of zebras and other large animals, African dung beetles are busy rolling balls to burial sites.

Temperate Forests and Fields

Hemlocks, maples, oaks, white pines, hickories, and tulip trees are the most important plants in the temperate forests of North America. Nestled between the cold regions to the north and the hot equator to the south, these forests have warm summers and cool winters. Insects that live in this in-between environment must survive long periods of cold weather, complete with ice and snow.

To survive the winter season, most insects spend three to six months in a state of inactivity or suspended animation. Queen wasps are the only wasps to survive the winter. After hibernating in holes or old nests, queens emerge to start new colonies in the spring.

Mourning cloak and question mark butterflies are also able to survive the winter as adults. Question marks have two distinct forms. You'll see question marks with dark hindwings only during the summer. Question marks with reddish brown and black-spotted wings survive the winter. You can see them only in the fall and spring.

Other butterflies, such as swallowtails, survive the winter as pupae that hatch in the spring. The silk cocoons of moths are also designed to protect pupae from winter weather. Sphinx moth caterpillars bury themselves and pupate underground to escape the frost and snow.

Most insect species endure the winter as eggs. Eggs are able to survive long periods of cold and drought, just like the seeds of trees.

When spring returns, it brings an explosion of insect life. A short walk among the trees may show you shimmery red-spotted purple butterflies. You may find carpenter ants slowly emptying a tree of its wood. Under logs you may discover bessybugs, ants, beetle larvae, and camel crickets. Buzzing your head could be two or three hungry deerflies. On the ground, dozens of tiny springtails may cover rocks or mats of pine needles.

Because the climate in temperate forests changes with the seasons, the insects in them must breed and multiply before the cold of winter returns.

The wild areas near your home are teeming with flying, crawling, and burrowing insects in all stages of development.

The Tropical Rain Forest

Where are the most kinds of insects found? As you travel south toward the humid forests near the equator, the numbers and variety of insects increases greatly. Insects flourish in the plant-filled tropical rain forests of the world.

Imagine you're walking through a rain forest under the huge trees. You notice a wood fairy butterfly fluttering down the trail on its transparent wings. On the trunk of a tree a red, black, and white harlequin beetle sits motionless with its long forelegs holding fast to the bark. But overall, you seem to see less life in the forest than in your neighborhood field.

But 100 feet (26 meters) above you are leafy treetops teeming with insects. Most insects of the rain forest live high in the trees. Wingless grasshoppers with long, fuzzy feet leap from leaf to leaf. Morphos butterflies glide over the canopy. Bright green and crimson bromeliad plants are filled with green roaches, mosquito larvae, and multicolored weevils. Trails of ants scurry from one place to the next.

Tropical entomologists and ecologists have collected huge numbers of species that live in the treetops. From their research, entomologists estimate that possibly ten million insect species live in the rain forests.

To truly appreciate the rain forests, you must go to the tropics and experience the unbelievable numbers of flowers, ferns, trees, monkeys, birds, and insects that live there. The variety is overwhelming. To get a taste of the insect jungle, visit insect zoos such as those on page 127.

WHERE THE WILD THINGS ARE

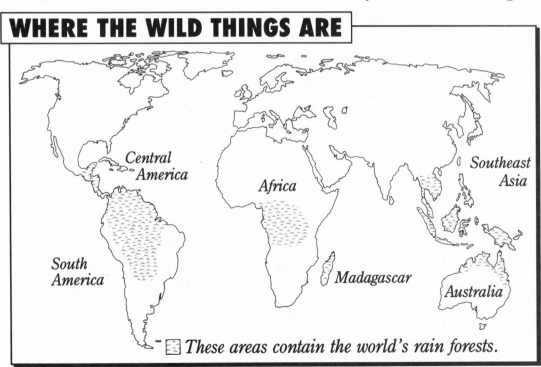

Central America

Africa

Southeast Asia

South America

Madagascar

Australia

These areas contain the world's rain forests.

More kinds of insects are found in the treetops of rain forests than in any other place in the world.

Pools of Predators

Looking at the surface of a quiet pond or lake, you may not realize that dozens of life-or-death struggles are taking place beneath the surface. Fish are the big predators and insects are an important part of their diets. There are also many insect predators lurking in the water. And in a few cases, the insects have turned the tables on their enemies, the fish.

Dragonflies flit and swerve above the water, hunting. Underwater, the dragonfly larvae hunt also. They live in weeds growing in the shallows. Dragonfly larvae are slow in the water, so they hunt by stealth. These larvae have extendable structures called *labrums* tucked under their heads. When a larva is close enough to its prey, it lunges forward with its labrum extended. The spines of the labrum pierce the prey and inject a venom into it. The labrum then pulls back and draws the captured prey into the larva's mouth. Dragonfly larvae eat all kinds of insects and even very small fish.

Many other predators patrol the water. Diving beetles trap air bubbles on their abdomens. They take these bubbles with them as an extra air supply so they can stay underwater longer. True to their name, backswimmers swim on their backs, using their legs like oars. They capture worms, insects, and other creatures by biting them with their long, tube-like mouths.

Water scorpions are odd, stick-like insects. They have long structures on their abdomens that reach to the surface and act as breathing tubes. Water scorpions grab passing prey with their crooked forelegs.

The largest aquatic insect predators are the giant water bugs. These three-inch (seven centimeter) beasts look like dead leaves when they are still. Giant water bugs feed on tadpoles and minnows, and can be pests in fish hatcheries.

ROW, ROW, ROW YOUR BEETLE

Diving beetles are master swimmers. These predators have flattened hind legs lined with hairs. These hairs remain stiff as the beetle rows itself forward. The hairs fold back on the return stroke. The legs act much like the oars of a boat.

Look for diving beetles in shallow water. Above water, you might spot a damselfly larva and a mayfly (top left) or a pond skater (middle).

Rippling with Insects

A mountain stream gurgling over rocks and drifting over flat stretches of water is usually full of insects. Streams rich with insect life are able to support populations of healthy trout, minnows, and amphibians.

Just sit by a stream and watch the large number of insects nearby. Midges (tiny flies), caddisflies, and mayflies zoom over streams looking for mates or laying eggs. Patiently parked on a leaf, a black-winged damselfly glistens green and blue in the sun.

Near the edge of a pool, black whirligig beetles paddle on top of the water like aquatic bumper cars. These scavengers have two sets of eyes—one set for seeing above the surface and another set for viewing below the surface.

Waterstriders skitter on the water's surface, too. Their front legs are shortened and angled to grab prey. Striders can walk on water with their other four legs, which are equipped with fine hairs. These hairs spread the waterstriders' weight and keep their legs from penetrating the water's surface.

Below the surface is a complex community of insects. Most are the larvae of mayflies, stoneflies, caddisflies, midges, and beetles. Each species has developed ways of coping with the fast-moving water. Mayfly nymphs have gills that they use like suction cups. They can move over the smoothest stones even in fast-flowing water.

Caddisfly larvae are unable to move quickly to food sources. Some species build cylindrical cases of pebbles, sand, and sticks around their bodies. Other species fish for their food. These caddisfly larvae string silken nets between rocks. As water rushes by, plant and animal material is trapped in the net. The larvae crawl from their protected hiding places to collect dinner.

The great abundance of insects in the stream helps feed colorful brook trout. Four-fifths of their food consists of insects caught underwater.

You might not expect it, but streams are full of insects skating on the water, swimming, and hiding under stones.

A Fall Floral Feast

In late summer and early fall, meadows turn yellow as the many species of goldenrod come into bloom. If you have hay fever, the pollen from these plants can make you sneeze. But for entomologists, these flowers are a great source of unusual insects. With a magnifying lens, you can observe a surprising number of insects feeding on goldenrod.

Close inspection of the flowers reveals a host of insects seeking nectar and pollen. Hover flies, banded yellow to imitate wasps, lap up the food. Black and yellow locust borers crawl through the flowers, wallowing in the pollen. These beetles help fertilize the goldenrod as they fly from one plant to another.

Such a gathering of insects does not go unnoticed by insect predators. Ambush bugs use the flowers as a place to hide and wait for unsuspecting insects. With strange ridges on their abdomens, these deadly hunters look much like pieces of the plants. They seize flies, wasps, and bees with their elbowed forelegs and drain their bodies with their sharp tubular mouths.

Ambush bugs are not the only predators found in the flowers. They compete with crab spiders, which are able to change their color to match the plants. Both kinds of creatures are capable of capturing insects twice their size.

Not all insect activity occurs on the flowers. Glancing down the stems of goldenrod, you can find odd grape-sized swellings. These growths are known as *galls* and are caused by wasps. Adult wasps lay eggs inside the stems of the plants. The larvae hatch and create chemicals that stimulate the plants to form hard swellings in the stems. At the centers of these balls are the fat larvae. The wasp larvae gain protection and a secure source of food by modifying the growth of the plants. The larvae eventually pupate, hatch, and escape the galls by boring holes in their sides.

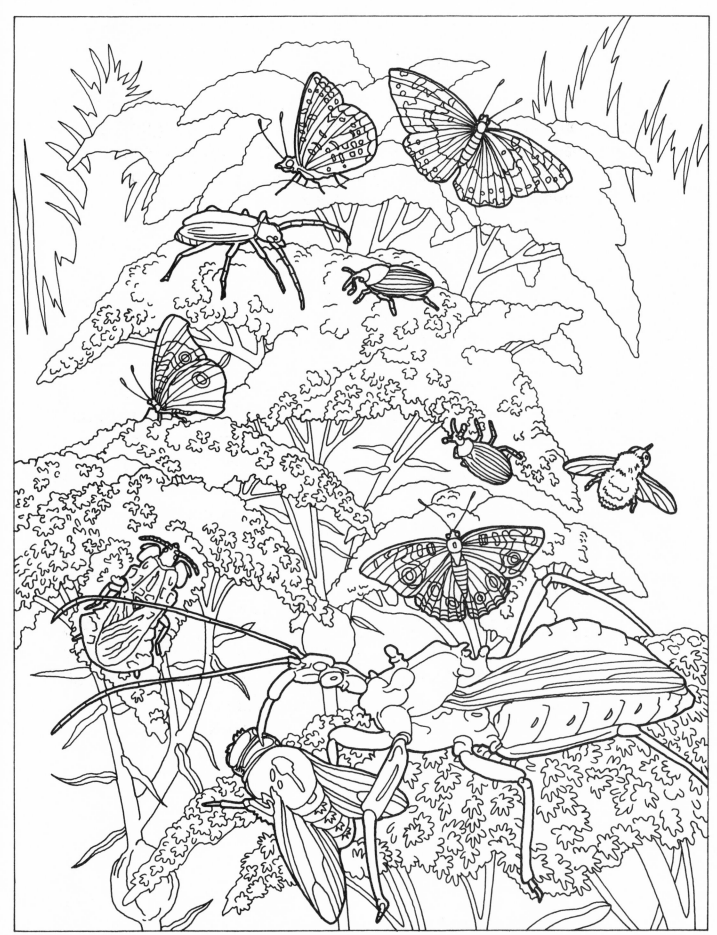

A clump of goldenrod flowers will attract dozens of kinds of feasting insects.

Sharing the Garden

If you've grown flowers or vegetables, you know that gardens grow more than just plants. Gardens are filled with insects. Most of these visitors are unwelcome and come to dine on your tomatoes, corn, carrots, and roses. Gardeners must become familiar with the insects that can infest and damage their plants.

Almost every plant has an insect that enjoys nibbling on its leaves, fruits, flowers, or roots. If you plant tomatoes, tomato hornworm caterpillars may appear. They can turn tomato plants into leafless stalks.

Gardeners who enjoy fresh corn on their tables may find a surprise hidden under the corn husks. Cutworm moth caterpillars attack the young corn kernels. Carrots and parsley are devoured by black swallowtail butterfly caterpillars. And potato plants are avidly consumed by the larvae of Colorado potato beetles.

Flower gardens are hit by insect infestations, too. By looking closely at the stems of roses, you may find sap-sucking insects called aphids. Chafer beetles dine on the petals and leaves.

Though it seems a garden is just a dinner table for feeding insects, a host of other insects aid gardeners. Ladybugs scurry up and down stems in search of aphids. Praying mantises stalk the foliage and snag unsuspecting grasshoppers, flies, and beetles. Hundreds of species of wasps and flies lay eggs on caterpillars, which then die before reaching maturity. And those insect relatives, the spiders, capture garden pests in their webs.

When raising vegetables and flowers, remember that your garden may contain helpful insects as well as troublesome ones. Before using pesticides, decide if it's worth killing all the insects in your garden in order to save a few plants. In most cases, natural predators or nonchemical methods can be used to limit losses in your garden.

Chomp, chomp, chomp. *If gardeners are not careful, Japanese beetles can destroy their roses.*

Locust Swarms

"Africa Plagued by Millions of Locusts!" Newspapers carry this headline every few years. The articles tell of huge swarms of insects sweeping across the land. Locust swarms are very destructive. Some have been so large and dense that they have been photographed from space by satellites! As they travel, locusts eat every piece of vegetation in their path. They devastate crops, leaving whole areas barren. This leads to the starvation of livestock and people.

A locust is a migratory grasshopper with the ability to fly great distances in order to find fresh plants to eat. During periods of drought, locust populations are low because they lack food. When there is plenty of rain over several years, the locusts build their populations. When their numbers grow large in certain areas, the young grasshoppers develop the urge to fly from their birthing grounds.

For locusts, the critical question is: "Where do we go to get fresh greenery?" The answer is: "Follow the rains." Where there's rain there are fresh plants. Scientists believe that locusts are able to detect weather conditions that produce rain. This sensitivity improves their chances of finding food. But it can also lead them to their deaths, as it did in 1989.

HUNGRY HOPPERS

In one bad outbreak, migratory locusts spread across Africa in only three years.

AFRICA

1929 1930 1931

In that year, huge swarms were sighted flying out to sea! It seems the locusts were attracted to storms over the ocean. These storms moved farther out to sea, strengthened, and became hurricanes that hit the Caribbean and the United States. The locusts were swept up by the storms. Although most of the locusts died, ten days after leaving Africa, a few arrived on the Caribbean islands of St. Vincent, St. Lucia, Dominica, and Grenada. These tough grasshoppers survived a 3,500 mile (5,600 kilometer) crossing of the Atlantic Ocean!

Swarming locusts form living clouds that can quickly consume tons of crops.

Millions of Moths

Dawn breaks at a small airport in eastern Pennsylvania. The loud roar of the engines drowns out the songs of birds. Large yellow cropdusters full of pesticides roar off the runway. These planes fly to areas of forests that are rapidly losing their leaves. Their target is the latest outbreak of a European insect invader, the gypsy moth.

Gypsy moths arrived in the United States from Germany in the early part of this century. Since that time, these moths have spread throughout New England and down the East Coast. Now they're spreading west. The caterpillars of these destructive insects enjoy eating a wide variety of trees. They like oak trees the best, but will even eat some species of pines.

Gypsy moths can destroy entire forests. Heavy infestations can completely strip all the leaves from the trees by June, making the countryside appear as if it was winter.

When you walk through a forest filled with gypsy moth caterpillars, there is no need to see them. If you listen, you will hear caterpillar droppings raining through the leaves. Some people say they can hear the sound of munching on quiet days.

In its natural habitat of Europe, a wide range of insects and birds prey upon the gypsy moth caterpillars and keep its numbers down. But elsewhere, gypsy moths don't face their old enemies. In the United States, only the shy cuckoo bird likes to eat the hairy caterpillars.

Forestry and insect scientists are introducing insects that attack and feed on gypsy moth caterpillars. Using insects to control other insects is called *biological control* and can be much safer than using pesticides. These scientists are raising large numbers of caterpillar-eating wasps and parasitic flies for release into gypsy moth infestations.

Even with the new biological controls and spraying, gypsy moths are here to stay. As new biological weapons are developed, everyone hopes to control this invader enough so that our forests are not stripped completely bare— just lightly nibbled.

Each gypsy moth caterpillar nibbles a little each day. When there are millions of caterpillars, acres of trees may die.

World Travelers

Our boats, trains, planes, and cars carry us to destinations throughout the world. Our transportation systems also allow insects to travel from one continent to another with ease. Many insect species have hitchhiked through the world and have colonized corners of the earth far from their original homes.

Often these hitchhikers arrive in food, plants, or even tourist trinkets made from natural products such as logs. For example, the now-common cabbage white butterfly and the bronzy-winged European skipper came by boat as larvae or pupae from Europe. Other species of insects, such as the destructive Japanese beetle, arrived by boat and plane and quickly multiplied in the United States, where their natural predators do not live.

Not all insect travelers need human help to reach new lands. Many species are able to travel under their own power. Butterflies such as the red admiral and the painted lady probably colonized the Americas by flying from Europe or Asia. The strong-flying monarch butterfly has managed to reach England and Australia from the United States and Mexico.

Flightless species let nature assist their travels. Crickets have used a slow but effective means to colonize the islands of the South Pacific. They take cruises on logs. Large storms on Pacific islands lift palm trees and their insect passengers out to sea. Occasionally these logs drift to other islands and new colonies of crickets become established.

The spread of insects has created a pest-control nightmare. California agricultural agents, for example, must carefully search for six-legged tourists. If you're arriving from a foreign country, these agents will search your car or baggage and confiscate any fruit, wood, dirt, and plants that could carry pests into the state. At airports, jets are inspected and fumigated for insects. Invaders like the Mediterranean fruit fly can threaten California's multi-billion dollar agricultural industry.

When traveling, make sure you're not carrying insects in your luggage. You may stop a major pest from entering the country.

Monarch butterflies fly south for the winter. Their migrations cover hundreds of miles. Newly hatched monarchs make the trip back north in the spring.

Uninvited Guests

Our homes provide year-round warmth, food, and shelter for us—and for other creatures. Many insects cannot resist such comfort and often share our houses with us. We try to evict these six-legged guests. Can you think of some insects that have appeared in your kitchen, basement, or bathroom?

Perhaps the most hated pests are roaches. Fast runners, these smooth-backed insects dash under counters and down holes as soon as you flick on the light. They eat almost anything, from shoe leather to glue. Few people realize that some cockroach species are able to fly!

House flies got their name because they're so difficult to keep out of the house. House flies are messy eaters and can carry a long list of diseases. They're a nuisance we all try to avoid.

In attics, clothes moth larvae eat woolen sweaters and coats. Silverfish are primitive insects with long feelers and bristly tails. They thrive in darkness and search for binding glue, wallpaper paste, and other starchy foods. In the back of the kitchen cabinet, mealworms feast in an old box of cereal someone left open.

To remove these pests, scientists have devised chemicals to protect our clothes, wood, and food. Chemical traps catch ants. Roach traps release scents that lure roaches to their deaths. Pesticide sprays and fogs are available in stores, and professional exterminators can deal with stubborn infestations.

In New York City, some people have found an unusual but effective way of dealing with the city's roach problem. They buy Tokay geckos. These tropical lizards, which grow up to 12 inches (30 centimeters) long, are hungry, fast, and can climb walls. During the day, the geckos hide and sleep. At night, they come out and hunt down roaches. These pets keep roaches away and make pesticides unnecessary.

Hungry geckos help keep some people's apartments pest-free.

Killer Bees

Are they coming? Do they kill? What can we do to stop them?

Already in the United States, African honeybees, nicknamed the "killer bees," have stung humans. Reportedly, people are killed by them in Central and South America each year. It seems that this more aggressive cousin of our much-loved honeybee is advancing into the states of the Southwest.

Because northern honeybees don't live well in very warm areas, African bees were taken to Brazil for research purposes. Unfortunately, several queens escaped and started new colonies in the wild. With their habit of moving their hives to new locations, the bees steadily moved through Central America at a rate of 100 miles (160 kilometers) per year.

African honeybees and common honeybees look almost exactly alike. The main difference between the two varieties is that African bees are very aggressive. African bees are quick to react to intruders. These bees mob enemies and can even kill them with an overdose of bee venom.

Fortunately, not all of the news is bad. "Killer" bees are being raised to produce honey. African bees are also resistant to parasites that are killing northern honeybee colonies. There is hope that through special breeding, this resistance can be passed on to our milder honeybees.

Despite the much-publicized risks, people in Africa and South America are managing to live peaceably with these bees. American bee specialists hope that the African bee expansion will be slowed by the cold winters of the United States. The negative effects of killer bees on our lives should be small.

INVASION OF THE KILLER BEES

UNITED STATES

MEXICO

1988 *Northern Mexico*

1986 *Southern Mexico*

1983 *Costa Rica*

1982 *Panama*

1980 *Colombia*

1975 *Surinam*

SOUTH AMERICA

Beekeepers who raise African bees must protect themselves. They always use smoke, which calms the bees.

Public Enemy Number One

The tiny mosquito is man's worst insect enemy. This is because mosquitoes transmit a wide range of diseases. During the construction of the Panama Canal in Central America, thousands of workers died of yellow fever carried by mosquitoes. And in their travels around the world during World War II, 500,000 military personnel contracted malaria from mosquito bites. Any area with fresh water—marshes, ponds, lakes, and swamps—can become infested with mosquitoes.

Equipped with large eyes and long tube-like mouths, female mosquitoes feed on blood. (Male mosquitoes do not drink blood.) Female mosquitoes can sense their victims through movement, heat, and even the gases they breathe out.

The females' needle-like mouths contain structures called *stylets*. One set helps the mouth puncture the skin of the prey. Another injects a chemical that keeps the blood from clotting. (This chemical is what makes mosquito bites swell and itch.) Yet another set of stylets withdraws the blood. Some species of mosquitoes require a meal of blood in order to lay their eggs, which are deposited in mats on the surface of calm water.

Approximately 2,500 species of these insects are known. More than two dozen transmit diseases harmful to humans. Some species seek other kinds of animals. In Hawaii, mosquitoes have infected the beautiful and endangered honeycreeper birds with a kind of bird malaria.

More money is spent studying and controlling mosquitoes than on any other pest. One old method for controlling mosquitoes involves draining swamps and lakes. In the 1940s and 1950s, chemicals such as DDT were used to control mosquitoes. DDT is now considered too dangerous to other kinds of wildlife, including humans, and is no longer used in the United States.

Today, researchers are concentrating on environmentally safe methods of control. One animal helping us fight the battle is the mosquitofish, a minnow that loves to eat mosquito larvae. Mosquitofish are placed into lakes where mosquitoes reproduce. They help control the insect population.

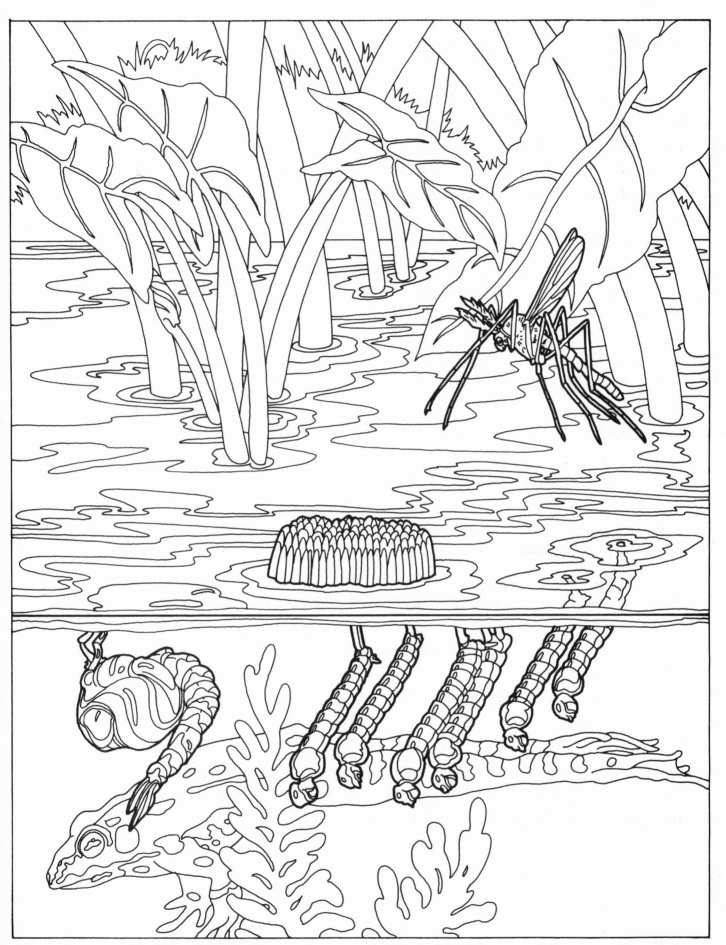

Mosquitoes need bodies of calm water to lay eggs (center). The larvae and fat pupae hang below the surface of the water and breathe through tubes on their abdomens.

Collecting Insects

Many people collect insects for fun. Through collecting, you can learn about insects' behavior, habitats, defense mechanisms, and their relationships with other animals.

Many amateur collectors become energetic professional naturalists who add insects to the amazing collections in museums. Some of these valuable collections contain 100,000 or more insects. These huge collections are valuable libraries of life that entomologists use to identify new species and learn about the habitats and evolution of insects. With millions of species of insects yet to be discovered, there is plenty of work to be done, even in the United States.

It's easy to start a collection. All you need are a cigar box, insect pins from a hobby store (regular pins are fine for large insects), a net, a jar, and a freezer. A good field guide will help you identify your specimens.

Collecting insects with a net can be both easy and challenging. If you sweep your net through the grass of a field, dozens of insects will fall in. Capturing a brightly colored dragonfly or butterfly is more difficult. It often helps to wait until a flying insect lands. If you miss, don't be discouraged.

Take your captured insects home to your freezer. Let them freeze for 48 hours. The rapid change in temperature will kill them quickly and cleanly, without the risks and mess of poisons.

Then let your specimens thaw. Carefully pin them through the thorax. Some winged insects will require special preparation. Butterflies, moths, and dragonflies can be placed on a mounting board with the wings held in a spread position with strips of paper. Preparation takes a little practice, so keep at it.

Use small pieces of paper as data tags. Record the date you caught the insect, where you found it, and your name:

Where found: _____

Habitat: _____

Date Caught: _____

Collector: _____

On a separate piece write the name of the insect. Place both tags on the pin. Though this information seems unimportant, it is this data that makes an insect collection valuable. An insect without this data is an insect without a story.

The miniature world of insects is all around us, waiting to be discovered. Insect collecting can reveal the secrets of these incredible creatures.

Night Prowling

While most other animals are asleep, the night is filled with active insects. Many insects remain hidden during the day and wait until evening to sing, feed, hunt, and mate. To witness these insects in an undisturbed setting, you must go on a night prowl.

For a night prowl, you'll want a headlamp. It will free your hands for other duties. If a headlamp is unavailable, use a flashlight. Always carry a second flashlight in case your first light fails. Armed with a net and a wide-mouthed collecting jar, you can easily collect dozens of insects in an evening. Ask a friend to prowl with you. He or she can help spot insects and help you find your way.

To enhance your chances of finding lots of insects, create a bait that you can smear on trees. A good recipe calls for stale beer, rotten bananas, and honey mixed into a liquid goo. Before sunset, walk along the route you plan to take and paint your bait onto three trunks. Put some near the ground and some at eye-level. The goo should have a strong odor—the stronger the better. Your smelly bait will attract a variety of visitors, including ants, crickets, beetles, and moths.

The secret lives of insects will be revealed to you at night. During your prowl, you may find butterflies resting under leaves, katydids singing in the grass, and caterpillars boldly dining on the plants in your garden. Your headlamp will cause many eyes to sparkle and glow. On the ground, the tiny white lights you may see are the reflective eyes of spiders.

MAKE A LIGHT TRAP

Have an adult put a fluorescent light on a side of your garage or house that faces a yard, field, or forest. Hang an old white sheet next to the light so that the light shines on the vertical white surface. Turn on the light after sunset. Go out every hour and see what insects come.

During a night prowl, your flashlight will reveal beautiful moths and other insects that hide during the day.

Raising Butterflies and Moths

To get a close-up view of how insects grow into adults, you can raise them from their larval stage. The most exciting and popular insects to rear are butterflies and giant silk moths. During the summer, hunt for their caterpillars.

You can create a cage for your caterpillars out of a box or fish tank. When you find a caterpillar, carefully note what kind of plant it's eating. You'll need to feed it that same kind of plant when you put it in your tank.

Then find a small jar. Fill the jar with water, cover it with several layers of foil, and insert sprigs of the caterpillar's foodplant through the foil and into the water. Place your caterpillar on the leaves and place the jar in the tank. Cover the tank with fine wire screen. The screen will keep your caterpillar in and parasitic wasps out.

Provide your caterpillar with a regular supply of fresh leaves. Also place dead leaves in the bottom of the tank. Lean a few sticks against the corners and walls of the cage. As the caterpillar eats, it will release droppings onto the floor of the cage. Clean the cage regularly.

COLLECTING TIPS

- *Be careful when collecting bees and wasps. Avoid these insects if you are allergic to them.*
- *Never collect more than a few specimens of the same kind from an area. Insects are an important part of the ecosystem.*
- *Visit a museum to see the incredible variety of insects found around the world. You'll find a list of insects zoos and exhibits on page 127.*

Eventually the caterpillar will stop eating and begin wandering about the cage. At this time, it's searching for a suitable place to make a cocoon. When it finds a suitable branch, the caterpillar will start weaving a silken case around itself. Some caterpillars prefer to make cocoons in the leaves on the bottom of the tank.

Keep the cocoon in the cage until it hatches. Some caterpillars stay in their cocoons for months and months. Eventually, your cocoon will split open and a shriveled moth or butterfly will crawl free. When its wings expand and dry, remove the covering from your cage and set your butterfly or moth free.

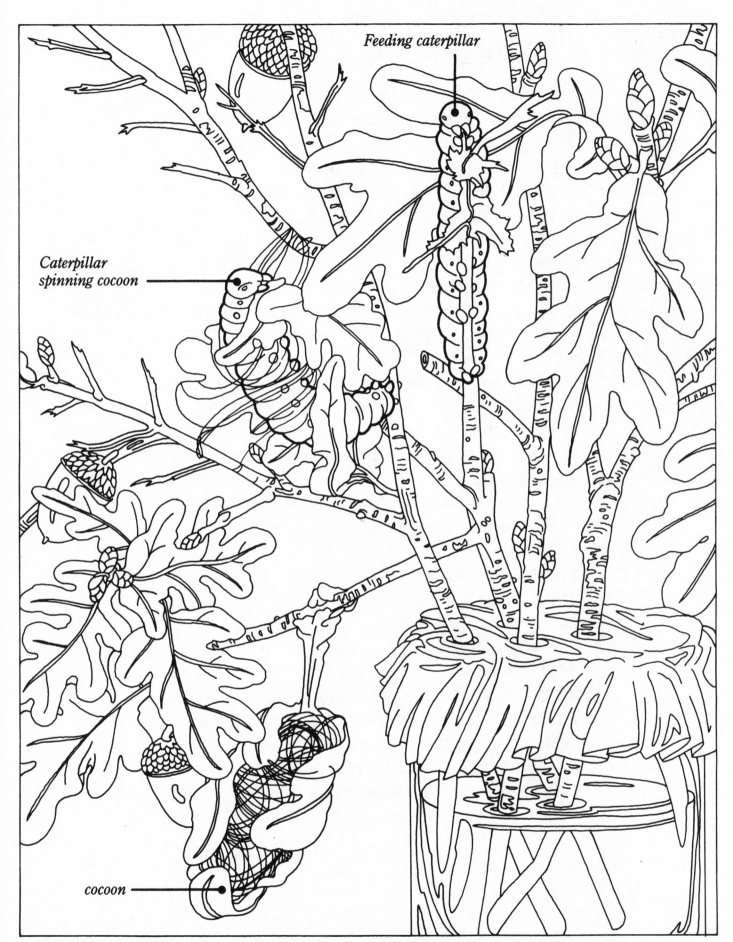

Feeding caterpillar

Caterpillar
spinning cocoon

cocoon

Give your caterpillars fresh green leaves daily until they weave their cocoons.

Butterfly Gardening

Raising butterflies and moths in captivity is the best way to observe their life cycles. However, the most enjoyable way of watching insects is in their natural habitat, the outdoors. One way to attract insects to your home is to plant a butterfly garden in your backyard or windowbox. By selecting certain species of flowers and plants, you can make your garden come alive with tiger swallowtails, sulphurs, skippers, and other beautiful butterflies.

To plant a garden attractive to flying insects, remember that butterflies seek sources of nectar in warm sunny areas. They are especially attracted to purple, white, and yellow. (Red flowers will bring hummingbirds.) Large butterflies will sip nectar from deep tubular flowers, such as lilacs and bush honeysuckle. Smaller species prefer large clumps of small flowers including yarrow, daisies, and boneset.

Each species has a menu of preferred flowers. Monarchs love phlox, goldenrod, and of course, milkweed. Great spangled fritillaries prefer purple thistle. A plant called butterfly bush is one of the most popular butterfly attractors. Its purple and white flowers can become covered with thirsty swallowtails and skippers.

The flowers you plant for butterflies may be visited by moths at night. Hummingbird and bumblebee moths enjoy feeding at stands of pale blue delphinium and pink honeysuckle flowers. These sphinx moths hover like bees. Tomato hornworm sphinx moths are attracted to petunias. These skillful fliers will arrive at dusk and sip nectar from deep tube-shaped flowers.

As you create your butterfly garden, also include food plants for caterpillars. This helps ensure a steady stream of adults for your garden. Good plants include milkweed (to attract monarchs), willow (for viceroys, red-spotted purples, white admirals, and mourning cloaks), and turtlehead (for Baltimore checkerspots). Parsley can attract black swallowtails.

A butterfly garden can regularly attract more than 30 species to your yard. And in addition to colorful butterflies and moths flying in and out, your garden will be filled with beautiful flowers and plants all the time.

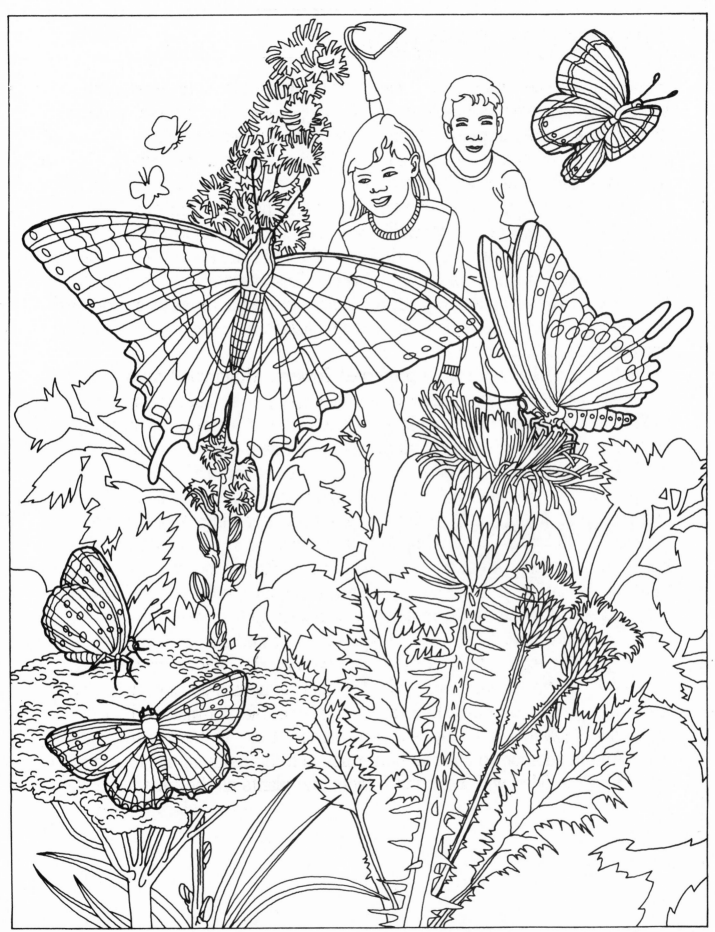

You can add living color to your garden by planting butterfly-attracting plants.

Saving the Insects

In the hills near Oakland, California flew rare blue butterflies called Xerces blues. With gray undersides and sky-blue uppersides trimmed in black, these interesting little insects were found only on a few areas. In the late 1940s, the construction of new houses destroyed their habitat. Soon after, the Xerces blues were declared extinct.

As you now know, insects can only survive if they have the right kinds of food. Human activity can destroy their homes and the land they rely on. While species do become extinct in the United States, it's in the rainforests of South America where most of the world's insects are disappearing forever. As the forests are logged, cut, and burned for farming, countless numbers of insects and their host plants vanish daily.

Often insects and other small animals such as snails, crabs, and worms are not considered important enough to protect. In their own ways, they're as important to the environment as elephants, pandas, and condors.

To help save these forgotten animals, the Xerces Society was formed to identify and help protect endangered insect species. This conservation organization promotes the protection of insects through the preservation of their habitats, the promotion of butterfly gardening and butterfly watching, and public education.

As you begin to appreciate the importance and beauty of insects, consider joining one of the many societies and associations committed to the protection and study of nature and insects. By becoming a member, you'll have access to a great many publications, field trips, equipment, and people who can help you learn more about the wild and wonderful world of insects.

ORGANIZATIONS AND SOCIETIES

American Entomological Society
1900 Race Street
Philadelphia, PA 19103
(215) 561-3978

Young Entomologists Society
International Headquarters
1915 Peggy Place
Lansing, MI 48910
(517) 887-0499

Xerces Society
10 Southwest Ash Street
Portland, OR 97204
(503) 222-2788

California
Xerces
blue

Spanish
moon moth

Indonesian
glass swallowtail

Queen
Alexandra's
birdwing

regal
fritillary

Philippine
swallowtail

Homerus
swallowtail

Just like elephants and eagles, many butterflies are in danger of extinction. But you can help preserve their habitats.

FOR FURTHER READING

General

Insects (Golden Guide series). Clarence Cottam and Herbert S. Zim. New York: Western Publications, 1987.

Insect (Eyewitness Books series). Laurence Mound. New York: Alfred A. Knopf, 1990.

A Guide to Observing Insect Lives. Donald W. Stokes. Boston: Little, Brown and Company, 1983.

Butterfly Gardening: Creating Summer Magic in Your Garden. Xerces Society Staff. San Francisco: Sierra Club Books, 1990.

Field Guides

Familiar Butterflies of North America (Audubon Pocket Guide series). Richard K. Walter. New York: Alfred A. Knopf, 1990.

A Field Guide to Insects. Donald J. Borror and Richard E. White. Boston: Houghton Mifflin Company, 1970.

Simon and Schuster's Guide to Insects. Ross H. Arness, Jr. and Richard L. Jacques, Jr. New York: Simon and Schuster, 1981.

INSECT ZOOS AND EXHIBITS

Insect Zoo
Smithsonian Institution
National Museum of Natural History
Tenth and Constitution Ave., N.W.
Washington, D.C. 20560

Academy of Natural Sciences
19th and the Benjamin Franklin Parkway
Philadelphia, PA 19103
(215) 299-1020

World of Insects Exhibit
Cincinnati Zoo
3400 Vine Street
Cincinnati, OH 45220
(513) 281-4701

Butterfly Exhibit
Marine World Africa–USA
Marine World Parkway
Vallejo, CA 94589
(707) 643-6722

Butterfly World
Trade Winds Park South
3600 West Sample Road
Coconut Creek, FL 33073
(305) 977-4400

Day Butterfly Center
Callaway Gardens
Pine Mountain, GA 31822
(404) 663-2281

The Running Press Start Exploring™ Series

Color Your World

With crayons, markers and imagination, you can recreate works of art and discover the worlds of science, nature and literature.

Each book is $8.95 and is available from your local bookstore. If your bookstore does not have the volume you want, ask your bookseller to order it for you (or send a check/money order for the cost of each book plus $2.50 postage and handling to Running Press).

START EXPLORING™ titles:

Oceans
by Diane M. Tyler and James C. Tyler, Ph.D.
Masterpieces
by Mary Martin and Steven Zorn
Forests
by Elizabeth Corning Dudley, Ph.D.
Gray's Anatomy
by Freddie Stark, Ph.D.
Space
by Dennis Mammana
Bulfinch's Mythology
by Steven Zorn
Insects
by George S. Glenn, Jr.